Easy Spicy Chicken Recipes AND Recipe Workbook

SPICY CHICKEN RECIPES FOR YOU TO TRY AND A WORKBOOK TO KEEP NOTE OF YOUR COOKING EXPERIMENTS. COMPANION BOOK TO EASY SPICY CHICKEN

JOSEPH VEEBE

This Recipe Book and Journal Belongs To

Other Books in this Series:

TABLE OF CONTENTS

CHAPTER 1. INTRODUCTION

INTRODUCTION

Humans have used spices from the beginning of time. One can find references to various spices in ancient scripts such as the Old Testament, Bhagavad-Gita, and other writings. Ancient Egyptians, Chinese, Indians, Arabs, Greeks, and Romans have all used spices for various purposes, from cooking to food preservation and as medicine. There were many things that attracted humans to the use of spices – their aroma, their distinct taste and ability to flavor food, their color, and last but not least their medicinal properties. Spices also helped early humans to preserve food and other things. Archeologists discovered the use of spices as preservatives or offerings in ancient Egyptian tombs and in other excavations. There are records of many civilizations around the world using herbs and spices for common ailments such as wound healing, fever, microbial infections, and such.

In modern cooking, spices are used not only to flavor food but also for their health benefits. The recipes included in this book healthy and made out of fresh ingredients – no processed or preserved ingredients. Most of the recipes are quick and easy and takes an average of 20-25 minutes to prepare. I have not used a rigid format for these recipes. You can vary the measurements to get it a low, medium, or high level of spice. I also give you optional ingredients and alternate ways of cooking (stovetop, instant pot, air fryer, oven, etc.). Consider these as more of recipe ideas and you can be creative in using less or more spices and also using alternate ingredients to create a slightly different dish out of the same recipe idea.

HEALTH BENEFITS OF SPICES

Spices and herbs used in recipes described in this book have many health benefits. Some of them are listed below.
- Antioxidant properties
- Anti-inflammatory properties
- Anti-cancer properties
- Anti-fungal, anti-microbial, anti-viral
- Help the immune system and fight infections.
- Lower blood pressure
- Lower cholesterol
- Lower diabetes
- Improve circulation.
- And many others

Spices and herbs, if used correctly, could improve overall health and help fight many health conditions in a natural and supplemental fashion to modern treatments.

ABOUT THIS BOOK

Do you like spicy dishes? Do you like Chicken? Do you like to experiment in the Kitchen? If so, this is a perfect recipe workbook for you. Companion book to *Easy Spicy Chicken.*

This book contains all the recipes listed in *Easy Spicy Chicken* but organized as workbook to encourage you to try the chicken recipes and take notes.

This book intended as a recipe-notebook that includes several recipes for you to experiment and take notes on your experiments for future reference and fine tuning of your culinary creations using these recipes. Each recipe is followed by notes pages for you to document your cooking experiment/tasting experience. There are also spaces for you to document your own favorite spicy chicken recipes or a family (or mom/grandma/dad/grandad recipes). I hope that you can use this book and notes as a record of your kitchen exploits and may even gift to your kids who are starting to explore cooking on their own such as going off to college or moving to their own homes.

Recipes in this book are not a collection of authentic dishes, but a spicy version of chicken recipes that are easy to make and 100% healthy and flavorful. Ingredients used are mostly natural without any preserved or processed foods. Most of these recipes include tips and tricks to vary and adapt to your taste of spice level or make with some of the ingredients you like other than the prescribed ingredients in the recipes. There are about 50 recipes in the book with ideas to make another 50 or even more with the suggestions and notes included with many of the recipes. Cooking does not have to be prescriptive but can be creative. I invite you to try your own variations and apply your creativity to cook dishes that are truly your own. Please see my book "Beginner's Guide to Cooking with Spices" to find out many health benefits of individual spices, and also tips and tricks in using these.

Notes:

CHAPTER 2. BAKED, GRILLED AND BARBEQUED CHICKEN

CHICKEN KEBABS #1

Ingredients
- 2 boneless chicken breasts cut into 1 inch cubes
- 3 tablespoon olive oil
- 1 medium red onion cut into chunks
- 1 red bell pepper cut into 1 inch squares
- 1 teaspoon curry powder
- ½ teaspoon black pepper powder
- ¼ teaspoon dried rosemary flakes
- ½ tsp salt or to taste
- 2 tablespoon red wine
- 2 tablespoon lemon juice
- ¼ cup coriander leaves
- 1 lemon cut into wedges

Method
1. Mix wine, lime, 2 tablespoon olive oil, salt, curry powder, pepper powder, and dried rosemary. Add chicken, bell pepper and onions, mix well so that they are well coated. Refrigerate for 2-3 hrs. or overnight.
2. Thread chicken, bell pepper, and onion on wooden skewers (soaked in water prior to use). Grill for 20-25 minutes or until chicken is cooked turning once after 12 minutes.
3. Sprinkle with finely chopped cilantro, 1 tablespoon olive oil. Squeeze lemon wedges over chicken pieces.

My Recipe Notes

Result: Loved it ♥   Okay ☑   Not for me ☒

Spice Level: Too Spicy 😖   Just Right 🙂   Not Spicy Enough 😎

Date(s):

Comments:

CHICKEN KEBABS #2

Ingredients
- 2 boneless chicken breasts cut into 1 inch cubes
- 1 tablespoon olive oil
- 1 teaspoon cumin powder
- ½-1 teaspoon chili powder
- 1 teaspoon coriander powder
- 2 teaspoon ginger-garlic paste
- ½ cup Greek yogurt
- ½ tsp salt or to taste

Method
1. Mix all ingredients in a bowl and make sure chicken pieces are coated well. You can use a fork to prick chicken pieces so some of the marinade gets inside the pieces. Refrigerate overnight.
2. Pre-heat oven to 400 degrees. Bake for 30 minutes or until chicken is cooked. Turn over after 15 minutes.

Serve as is or with tomato ketchup or your favorite chutney.

Recipe Notes:
1. As in the previous recipe, the chicken may be grilled in a skewer.

My Recipe Notes

Result: Loved it ♥   Okay ☑   Not for me ☒

Spice Level: Too Spicy 😎   Just Right ☺   Not Spicy Enough 😎

Date(s):

Comments:

CHICKEN TIKKA

Ingredients

- 2 boneless chicken breasts cut into 1-inch cubes
- 3 tablespoon olive oil
- 1 medium red onion cut into chunks (optional)
- 1 red bell pepper cut into 1-inch squares (optional)
- 1 teaspoon cumin powder
- ½ teaspoon turmeric powder
- ½ -1 teaspoon garam masala
- 1 teaspoon Kashmiri chili powder
- 2 teaspoon ginger garlic paste
- ½ tsp salt or to taste
- 2 tablespoon lemon juice
- ¼ cup Greek yogurt

Method

1. Mix all the ingredients with chicken and optional bell pepper and onions. Marinate overnight or at least 2-3 hours in the fridge.
2. Preheat oven to 400 degrees. Thread chicken, bell pepper, and onion on wooden/metal skewers. Grill for 20-25 minutes or until chicken is cooked turning once after 12 minutes.

Recipe Note:

1. If using wooden skewers, soak it in water for an hour so they do not get burned in the oven.

My Recipe Notes

Result: Loved it ♥   Okay ☑   Not for me ☒

Spice Level: Too Spicy 😝   Just Right ☺   Not Spicy Enough 😎

Date(s):

Comments:

_____

_____

_____

_____

_____

_____

_____

_____

_____

_____

_____

_____

_____

_____

_____

_____

EASY AIR FRIED CHICKEN

This is a 15-minute recipe for making air fried chicken cubes that can be served as a party appetizer or a snack item.

Ingredients
- 1 lb. chicken breasts cut into 1-inch cubes
- ½ teaspoon turmeric powder (optional)
- ½ teaspoon chili powder (optional)
- ½ teaspoon black pepper powder
- 1 tablespoon coconut or olive oil
- 1 tablespoon lime juice
- ½ teaspoon salt or to taste

Method
1. Mix chicken with all the ingredients in a large enough bowl and set aside for 15 minutes (or more)
2. Air fry for 10-15 minutes @ 400 degrees or until done, tossing them over midway.

Recipe notes:
1. The optional ingredients make the chicken spicy.
2. Instead of turmeric and chili powder separately, you could try with 1 teaspoon (or more) of other spice mixes such as tandoori chicken masala, curry masala or garam masala. Each one will give you a different taste.

My Recipe Notes

Result: Loved it ♥   Okay ☑ Not for me ☒

Spice Level: Too Spicy 😄 Just Right 😊 Not Spicy Enough 😎

Date(s):

Comments:

EASY AIR FRIED CHICKEN & VEGETABLES

This recipe cooks both chicken and vegetables together and you get both your veggies and chicken in 15 minutes.

Ingredients

- 1 lbs. chicken breasts cut into 1-inch cubes
- 1-2 tsp garam masala/chicken masala/curry powder
- 2 tsp ginger-garlic paste
- 1 tablespoon coconut or olive oil
- ½ cup non-fat yogurt
- ½ red and ½ green bell pepper cut into 1 inch pieces
- ½ Italian squash cut into ¼ inch rounds
- ½ teaspoon salt or to taste

Method

1. Mix chicken and veggies with all the ingredients in a large enough bowl and set aside for 15 minutes or more (refrigerate overnight will marinate better)
2. Set the air fryer to 15 minutes @ 400 degrees and add chicken. Add vegetables ½ way through frying or at 8 minutes.

Recipe notes:

1. Instead of garam/chicken masala, you can try chili, turmeric, coriander, cumin powders (suggest 1:1:2:2 ratio or ½ tsp chili, ½ turmeric, 1 tsp coriander, 1 tsp cumin)
2. You can use chicken drumsticks or thighs with the same recipe. If using drumsticks or thighs, make some cuts into the meat so the spices will get inside and also marinate for a longer time. You may also have to cook for 3-4 minute extra in the air fryer as they may take more time than smaller chicken cubes.

My Recipe Notes

Result: Loved it ♥   Okay ☑   Not for me ☒

Spice Level: Too Spicy 😌   Just Right 🙂   Not Spicy Enough 😎

Date(s):

Comments:

EASY CHILI CHICKEN WINGS

This is an easy recipe for making chicken wings as a snack or appetizer.

Ingredients
- 2 lbs. chicken wings (about 15 wings)
- 1-2 teaspoon Kashmiri chili powder
- 1-1/2 cup chili sauce
- ½ teaspoon salt or to taste
- 2 teaspoon oregano
- ½ teaspoon black pepper powder

Method
1. Mix all the ingredients in a bowl and marinate chicken for 1-2 hours in the refrigerator.
2. Bake in an oven at 400 degrees for 30-40 minutes or until cooked or grill them on an open grill.

Recipe note:
1. Red chili sauce is easier to find in grocery stores. If you like to make them at home, a simple recipe is to mildly roast red chilies and grind it with sautéed onions, garlic, and ginger with 2-3 teaspoons of vinegar of your choice.
2. Instead of chili sauce, you can try 1-2 teaspoon curry powder, garam masala, tandoori masala, or simply a mix of 1 teaspoon chili powder and half teaspoon turmeric. Each one of this will give you a different flavor/taste.
3. You can try the same recipe without oregano and see how you like it.
4. Try brushing the wings with unsweetened condensed milk midway and at the end and see if this is something you would like.

My Recipe Notes

Result: Loved it ♥   Okay ☑   Not for me ☒

Spice Level: Too Spicy 😝   Just Right 🙂   Not Spicy Enough 😎

Date(s):

Comments:

SPICY ROASTED CHICKEN

Ingredients

- 2 tbsp coconut oil (olive oil or vegetable oil can be used as well)
- 6-8 chicken thighs or drumsticks with skin
- ½ -1 tsp turmeric powder
- ½ tsp black pepper powder
- 1 tsp coriander powder
- ½ - 1 tsp chili powder
- 2 tbsp tomato paste
- 2 tablespoon fresh lemon juice
- 2-inch piece of ginger root peeled
- Salt to taste
- 6 cloves of garlic peeled

Optional Ingredients

- 1 lemon cut into 6-8 slices
- ½ onion sliced
- ¼ cup cilantro chopped

Method
1. Put all the ingredients (except chicken) into a food processor and make it a smooth paste
2. Wash chicken thighs/drumsticks and use a knife to make cuts/piercing all over the chicken so that marinade gets inside the chicken meat.
3. Rub the spice paste thoroughly into the chicken and under the skin. Put the chicken and any remaining paste into a Ziplock bag and shake well. Refrigerate overnight.
4. Heat oven to 400 degrees. Transfer chicken to a roasting pan and roast for 40-45 minutes or until done. Turning midway through roasting.
5. Garnish with cilantro, lemon wedges, and onions.

My Recipe Notes

Result: Loved it ♥   Okay ☑   Not for me ☒

Spice Level: Too Spicy 😆   Just Right 🙂   Not Spicy Enough 😎

Date(s):

Comments:

_____

_____

_____

_____

_____

_____

_____

_____

_____

_____

_____

_____

_____

_____

_____

_____

_____

CHICKEN TANDOORI

Tandoori chicken is an Indian dish that is marinated in yogurt and spices and cooked in clay oven. It invariably uses a ginger-garlic paste as part of the marinade. Below is a variation of tandoori chicken but cooked on a grill.

Ingredients
- 2-3 lbs. skinless chicken drumsticks or thighs/alternatively boneless chicken breast cut into pieces.
- 2-3 tsp ginger-garlic paste (see earlier instructions to make it or use store-bought)
- 1 cup low-fat yogurt
- 1 tsp chili powder
- ¼ tsp turmeric powder
- 3 teaspoon tandoori masala (see note below)
- 1 lemon juiced
- 1 cup cilantro (to garnish)
- 2 lemons sliced (to garnish)
- 1 medium onion sliced into long pieces (optional)
- 1 teaspoon salt (or to taste)
- 1 teaspoon oil

Method

The first step is to prepare the marinade.

Marinade Method 1: Mix all the items for marinade (yogurt, chili, turmeric, tandoori masala, lemon juice, and ginger-garlic paste, salt) into a smooth thick marinade.

Marinade Method 2: Heat oil and fry chili powder, tandoori masala, and turmeric for 2 minutes. Switch the heat and let it cool down. Once cooled, add this to the rest of the ingredients of the marinade and mix well as in the previous step.

1. Put the chicken in a large freezer /Ziplock bag and add the marinade. You may want to use multiple freezer bags depending on the quantity but make sure to put sufficient marinade in each bag. Shake the bag well carefully so that the chicken is well coated with the marinade. Refrigerate for a minimum of 2 hrs. but preferably 12 hrs. or overnight.
2. When ready to cook, pre-heat oven to 400 degrees. Take the chicken out of the zip lock bags and carefully place the chicken on a wire rack on the baking dish. The baking dish may be lined with aluminum foil to collect any juice coming out of the chicken. Bake for 25 minutes. Open the oven and apply some oil using a brush on the surface of chicken pieces and turn them over. Bake for another 20 minutes or until cooked well and slightly charred. Take it out from the oven. Garnish with cilantro, lemon wedges, and onion slices.

Instead of oven, the marinated chicken may be barbecued or grilled on an open grill as well.

Note: You can substitute garam masala for tandoori masala. Both of these spice mixes are available in any south Asian store or in the spice section in many grocery stores. You can also make the spice mix by combining the following: 1 tsp coriander powder, 1 tsp pepper powder, 1 tsp cinnamon powder, 1 tsp turmeric powder, ½ tsp cardamom powder (or seeds), 1 tsp chili powder, ½ tsp nutmeg.

My Recipe Notes

Result: Loved it ♥   Okay ☑   Not for me ☒

Spice Level: Too Spicy 😆   Just Right 🙂   Not Spicy Enough 😎

Date(s):

Comments:

SPICED FRIED CHICKEN NUGGETS

This recipe is used to spice up chicken nuggets and make a quick appetizer for parties. The first time I tried this recipe was to use up leftover chicken nuggets in the freezer when kids got tired of chicken nuggets.

Ingredients

- 15-20 chicken nuggets – thawed and sliced lengthwise (long thin slices)
- ½ inch grated ginger
- 4 cloves of garlic chopped
- 1 tsp turmeric powder
- ½ -1 tsp curry powder (optional)
- 3 jalapenos chopped– seeds removed
- 2 large onions finely chopped
- ¼ cup cilantro
- 2 tsp olive oil
- Salt to taste (or avoid as chicken nuggets are already salted)
- 2 springs of green onions chopped
-
- 2 medium tomatoes chopped (optional #1)
- 2 tsp lemon juice (optional #2)

Method

1. Heat oil in a pan over medium heat, sauté onions, ginger, garlic, jalapenos, and green onions
2. Add turmeric and optional curry powder. Sauté for about a minute until spices become fragrant.
3. Add optional tomatoes and mix well, let the tomatoes cook (1-2 minutes)
4. Now add the sliced chicken nuggets and mix well so the chicken is coated with the spices.
5. Add cilantro. Mix well and serve.
6. If you skipped step 3 (adding optional tomatoes), you could lemon juice and mix before serving.

Recipe Notes

1. Instead of chicken nuggets, you may use frozen chicken tenders, or chicken patties. Just thaw them and then slice them into thin slices before using in the recipe.
2. Instead of tomatoes, you may use ½ cup salsa and see if you like this variation better than either tomato or lemon juice one.
3. This may be used as a filling in wraps or burritos. Add some cheese and/or sour cream as you like for the filling.

My Recipe Notes

Result: Loved it ♥   Okay ☑   Not for me ☒

Spice Level: Too Spicy 😆   Just Right 🙂   Not Spicy Enough 😎

Date(s):

Comments:

10 MINUTE SPICY FRIED CHICKEN

My daughter loves this recipe. This is very spicy, and I can make it quickly for her. Uses cooked or rotisserie chicken meat.

Ingredients
- 2 cups of rotisseries chicken meat – shredded or cut into pieces
- 1 tsp chili powder – divided
- ½ turmeric powder
- ½ tsp meat/garam masala (optional)
- ¼ cup red onions finely chopped
- ¼ cup cilantro chopped (optional)
- ¼ cup salsa (optional)
- 1 tbsp olive oil
- Salt to taste

Method
1. Sprinkle ½ tsp chili powder on the shredded chicken. Mix well and set aside.
2. Heat oil in a pan over medium heat, sauté onions, and spices.
3. Add chicken, optional salsa and mix well so the spices with hot oil sticks to chicken along with sautéed onions.
4. Garnish with cilantro and serve.

Recipe Notes
1. You can add ginger-garlic paste or grated ginger and chopped garlic in step 2.
2. Try other herbs such as oregano, chives or green onions (add in step 2)
3. If you like it even more spicy, try more chili powder or add a finely chopped jalapeno or green chili.
4. You can increase onions to 1 cup if you like or add tomatoes instead of optional salsa.
5. You can also use fresh chicken. In this case, cut into small pieces so it fries and cooks quickly.
6. Chicken may be marinated for longer period of time, as well as adding additional ingredients you like/prefer – such as lime juice, yogurt, ginger garlic paste, etc.
7. This fried chicken may be used in tacos, burritos, quesadilla, pizza, salads, and many more dishes.

My Recipe Notes

Result: Loved it ♥   Okay ☑   Not for me ☒

Spice Level: Too Spicy 😎   Just Right ☺   Not Spicy Enough 😎

Date(s):

Comments:

CHICKEN 65

Chicken 65 is deep-fried chicken dish that is popular south India. It is believed to be originated in Chennai (Madras), India. Some believed it has 65 ingredients and some say it is marinated for 65 days, whatever the case may be, it was a brilliant marketing effort from the hotel who served it first. Chicken 65 has become one of the more popular Indian chicken dishes today.

Ingredients

- 1.5 lbs. chicken breast cut into bite size cubes
- ½ - 1 tsp cumin powder
- 2-3 tsp Kashmiri chili powder
- ½ tsp turmeric
- 3 tsp coriander powder
- ½ tsp black pepper powder (optional)
- 2 tsp ginger-garlic paste (optional)
- ½ cup low-fat yogurt
- Salt to taste
- ½ cup oil to fry chicken

- ½ cup tomato ketchup
- 5-6 garlic cloves chopped
- 3-4 jalapenos chopped
- 1 tbsp coconut or olive oil
- 2-3 whole red chilies (optional)
- 1 spring curry leaves /1/2 cup cilantro

Method

1. In a large enough bowl, mix chili powder, coriander powder, turmeric powder, pepper powder, salt, and optional pepper powder and ginger-garlic paste and yogurt. Add chicken and mix it well so the chicken is coated with the marinade. Marinate for 5-6 hours or overnight.
2. Heat oil in frying pan and shallow fry the marinated chicken both sides till cooked and golden in color. Drain the fried chicken on a paper towel.
3. Heat 1 tbsp oil in a large enough pan, sauté garlic, jalapenos, whole red chilies and curry leaves. Add fried chicken and tomato ketchup. Toss well and cook for 2-3 more minutes mixing well until any water is evaporated and chicken pieces are dry.
4. Garnish with chopped green onions and/or lemon wedges and serve.

Recipe Notes:

1. You can adjust the amount of spices to control the spice/heat level
2. Instead of curry leaves, you may use cilantro.
3. To make the chicken crispy, add ½ cup of use corn flour, gram flour or rice flour while preparing the marinade.
4. You can try the recipe without yogurt and see if you like it better than with yogurt.
5. You can add lemon juice or vinegar while marinating instead of yogurt or in addition to yogurt.

My Recipe Notes

Result: Loved it ♥   Okay ☑   Not for me ☒

Spice Level: Too Spicy 😅   Just Right 🙂   Not Spicy Enough 😎

Date(s):

Comments:

CHAPTER 3. SPICY CHICKEN CURRY RECIPES

SPICY CHICKEN MASALA

Ingredients
- 2 lbs. boneless chicken breast cut into 1-inch cubes, washed with salt and pinch of turmeric
- 4 tablespoon coconut oil (olive oil or vegetable oil can be used as well)
- 3 medium red onions chopped
- 4 medium tomatoes chopped
- ½ tsp turmeric powder
- 2-4 tsp coriander powder
- ½ - 1 tablespoon chili powder
- 1 teaspoon fresh black peppercorns
- 1 teaspoon cumin seeds
- ½ teaspoon mustard seeds (optional)
- 2-inch ginger peeled
- 6-10 cloves of garlic peeled
- ½ tsp salt or to taste
- ½ cup cilantro chopped
- 2 springs curry leaves
- 1 can (14/16 oz) coconut milk (optional)

Method
1. In a food processor, make a paste of all the spices, ginger and garlic.
2. Heat oil and sauté onions, curry leaves and the spice paste and cook them for about 2-3 minutes or until the spices are cooked and fragrant.
3. Add the chicken pieces and mix well so that chicken pieces are well coated with the spice mix.
4. Add tomatoes. Mix well and cover and cook for 15 minutes or until chicken is cooked and tender. Add ½ cup water if tomatoes and chicken are not generating enough water when cooked.
5. Add optional coconut milk and simmer for 3-4 minutes.
6. Garnish with cilantro

Serve with rice or bread.
Recipe Notes:
1. Try the recipe without coconut milk and with coconut milk. You can make two different versions of the curry.
2. Try with whipping or heavy cream instead of coconut milk if you like the curry to be creamy but not coconut flavor.

My Recipe Notes

Result: Loved it ♥   Okay ☑ Not for me ☒

Spice Level: Too Spicy 😆 Just Right 🙂 Not Spicy Enough 😎

Date(s):

Comments:

CREAMY CHICKEN CURRY

Basic Ingredients

- 2 tablespoon coconut oil (olive oil or vegetable oil can be used as well)
- 1-1/2 lbs. boneless chicken breast cut into 1-inch cubes
- ½ tsp turmeric powder
- 1-2 tsp garam masala powder or curry powder
- 2-4 tsp coriander powder
- 2 tsp ginger garlic paste
- ½ tsp salt or to taste
- ¼ cup fresh cream
- 10-12 cashew nuts
- 1 cup low-fat yogurt
- 2 medium onions chopped

Optional Ingredients

- 1 Jalapeño pepper sliced into thin pieces
- ¼ cup cilantro chopped

Method

1. Sprinkle turmeric powder, coriander powder, garam masala powder and salt on the washed and cut chicken, mix well. Add ginger-garlic paste and yogurt and mix again. Let the chicken marinate for 1-2 hours (or overnight in the refrigerator)
2. Heat oil in pan, add onions and cashew nuts. Sauté until onions become translucent. Transfer into a food processor and make it a paste (both onions and cashew) and set aside.
3. Heat remaining oil in the same pan. Add marinated chicken and any juices. Cook on medium heat for about 5-6 minutes or until most of the water dries up.
4. Now the onion and cashew paste and jalapenos. Mix and cook until onions and all the spices are cooked well.
5. Add 1 cup of water. Cover and cook for 15 minutes or until chicken is cooked and tender.
6. Add cream and optional cilantro, mix well and simmer for 2-3 minutes.

Serve with rice or bread.

My Recipe Notes

Result: Loved it ♥   Okay ☑   Not for me ☒

Spice Level: Too Spicy 😊   Just Right 🙂   Not Spicy Enough 😎

Date(s):

Comments:

CHILI CHICKEN

Chili Chicken (or Chilli Chicken) is a popular Indo-Chinese chicken recipe that is sweet and savory. Chicken is marinated in a marinade made of ginger garlic paste, corn flour and eggs and deep fried in oil and then cooked with vegetables in a combination spices and sauces

Ingredients

- 2 lbs. chicken breast cut into 1-inch cubes
- 2 tsp ginger garlic paste
- ½ cup corn flour
- 1 egg beaten
- ½-1 teaspoon Kashmiri chili powder (optional)
- ¼ cup sliced jalapenos
- 1 tablespoon soy sauce
- 2 tablespoon vinegar
- 1 chopped up bell pepper (optional)
- ½ cup coconut oil (or vegetable oil)
- ¼ cup cilantro or chopped up spring onion to garnish (optional)
- ½ -1 cup water

Method

1. Combine eggs, corn flour, ginger-garlic paste, and optional Kashmiri chili powder in a bowl and mix well. Add sufficient water (½ cup or less should be enough) so that there is enough batter to coat all the chicken pieces. Mix well and refrigerate for 1-2 hours.
2. Heat oil in a pan and deep fry the marinated chicken in a couple of batches or a few pieces at a time. Transfer the fried chicken on a plate layered with tissue paper to absorb any excess oil.
3. Heat 1 tablespoon oil a separate pan (or the same pan in step 2 if it is clean enough) and sauté onions and optional bell pepper until onions become translucent and bell pepper tender (about 2-3 minutes)
4. Add fried chicken, vinegar, soy sauce and salt and mix well. Make sure that chicken and vegetables are well coated with the sauce.
5. Garnish with your choice of cilantro or spring onion and serve.

My Recipe Notes

Result: Loved it ♥   Okay ☑   Not for me ☒

Spice Level: Too Spicy 😆   Just Right 🙂   Not Spicy Enough 😎

Date(s):

Comments:

CHICKEN AND CASSAVA

Ingredients

- 3 lb. skinless chicken thighs or drumsticks
- 2 lb. cassava peeled, washed and cut into 1-inch pieces (frozen sliced cassava may be used as well)
- 2 tsp coconut oil (olive oil or vegetable oil can be used as well)
- 1/2 tsp turmeric powder
- 1-2 tsp black pepper powder
- 2 tsp coriander powder
- 2 large onion sliced
- 2-inch piece of ginger thinly sliced
- ½ - 1 tsp salt or to taste
- 2-3 medium tomato sliced
- 4-6 cloves of garlic crushed
- Cilantro – 1 cup (optional)
- ½ - 1 cup water/chicken stock/bone broth

Method

1. Sprinkle ½ teaspoon of turmeric powder, 1 tsp coriander powder, ½ tsp cumin powder and salt on the chicken, mix well and set aside for 20 minutes.
2. Heat oil in a pan; add onions, garlic and ginger. Stir until golden.
3. Add coriander powder, pepper powder and turmeric. Stir for 2-3 minutes.
4. Add tomato and mix well.
5. Add chicken and cassava. Add salt. Mix well. Transfer the contents to a pressure cooker or one pot. Add sufficient water/broth (usually ¾ of a cup) so that there is enough water to build steam in the cooker.
6. Set it to poultry and cook or cook high pressure for about 8 minutes.
7. Release steam naturally. Garnish with cilantro and serve.

Recipe Notes:

1. In most cases, water and juices from chicken and cassava are enough to pressure cook the dish. But while mixing and transferring the contents to the cooker, ½ cup - 1 cup water or chicken broth may be added to make sure there is enough water for pressure cooking.
2. The spices may be sautéed in an instant pot set to sauté mode or in a pressure cooker on an open stove. In that case, there is no need to transfer the contents from the sautéing pan to the pressure cooker.
3. Instead of a pressure cooker, a crockpot or a stovetop utensil may be used. In this case, cover the pot and cook on low-medium heat until the chicken is well cooked.
4. Alternatively, cassava and chicken may be cooked separately and mixed with spices. In this case, follow the steps below.
   a. Cook marinated chicken and set aside.
   b. Cook cassava with salt (boil with sufficient water, drain) and set aside.
   c. Follow steps 2,3 and 4 to make a cooked masala.
   d. Add cooked chicken, cassava, and mix well. Add cilantro, additional salt if needed, and serve.

My Recipe Notes

Result: Loved it ♥   Okay ☑   Not for me ☒

Spice Level: Too Spicy 😊   Just Right 🙂   Not Spicy Enough 😎

Date(s):

Comments:

SPINACH AND CHICKEN (CHICKEN SAAG/PALAK CHICKEN)

Ingredients

- 2 lbs. chicken breast cut into 1-inch pieces
- 4 cups of spinach washed and chopped
- 3 tsp coconut or olive oil
- 1/2 tsp cumin seeds
- 1/2 tsp cayenne powder (or chili powder)
- 1 medium onion chopped
- 1/2 tsp turmeric
- 1 tsp coriander powder
- 1 tsp cumin powder
- Salt to taste
- 2 green chilies seeds removed and chopped
- 1 inch ginger
- 6 cloves of garlic chopped
- 1 tablespoon lemon juice
- 2 pods of cardamom (optional)
- 1 cup water or 1 can coconut milk (optional)

Method

1. Mix all the spice powders (coriander, cumin, chili, and turmeric) with lemon juice, salt, and 1 tsp coconut oil. Add chicken pieces and mix so that the chicken pieces are covered with spices. Marinate for 1 hour or preferably overnight in the refrigerator.
2. Heat 1 tsp oil in a pan. Crackle cumin seeds. Add onions, ginger, garlic, green chilies, and cardamom. Sauté for 30 seconds and then add washed spinach and mix well.
3. Cook spinach for about 4-5 minutes covered or until spinach wilted sufficiently. Transfer to a blender and allow it to cool.
4. Add the rest of the oil to the pan and cook chicken with all the marinade/spices. Cover and cook it on medium heat for about 5 minutes.
5. Now blend the spinach with optional coconut milk. If you decide not to use coconut milk, it should be still fine. Add the blended spinach into the chicken and mix well.
6. Cover and simmer on low heat for 10 minutes or until chicken is cooked well and the dish is thick.

Variations to Saag Chicken Recipe

There are numerous variations to saag chicken recipe. Some alternative recipe ideas are listed below:

While *saag* chicken or *palak* chicken are prepared with spinach, the same recipe may be attempted with the following leafy vegetables or greens:

- Swiss chard (red or green)
- Dandelion greens
- Kale – all types
- Collard greens

- Beetroot greens
- Arugula
- Turnip Greens

Please note that some greens may take more time to wilt when cooked. So, adjust your time according to the type of green you are using.

As an alternative to cooking in a pan, you could steam the greens before blending.

In addition to the above ingredients, you may add 3-4 chopped up tomatoes along with spinach in step 3. This will be a different variation saag chicken.

Saag chicken may be made in an instant pot which will make it even more easy and quick. In this case, step 4 above is done in the sauté mode in the instant pot. After that add marinated chicken, blended spinach and mix well, close the lid and pressure cook for about 8 minutes.

My Recipe Notes

Result: Loved it ♥   Okay ☑   Not for me ☒

Spice Level: Too Spicy 😄   Just Right 🙂   Not Spicy Enough 😎

Date(s):

Comments:

Notes:

MINT CHICKEN

Ingredients

- 2 chicken breasts cut into 1-inch pieces
- 2 cups of mint washed and chopped
- 3 tsp coconut or olive oil
- 1 medium onion chopped
- 1/2 tsp turmeric
- 1 tsp coriander powder
- 1 tsp cumin powder
- 1 tsp black pepper powder
- ½ cup Greek yogurt
- Salt to taste
- 2 green chilies seeds removed and chopped (optional)
- 1 inch ginger
- 6 cloves of garlic chopped

Method

1. Mix all the spice powders (coriander, cumin, black pepper, and turmeric), salt, and yogurt. Add chicken pieces and mix so that the chicken pieces are covered with spices. Marinate for 30 minutes.
2. Puree onions, ginger and garlic and set aside.
3. Heat 2 tsp oil in a pan. Fry the marinated chicken pieces on both sides for about 4-5 minutes or until browned. Remove the chicken and let it sit.
4. To the same pan add the pureed onions, garlic, and ginger puree. Stir well so the onions are caramelized – about 3-4 minutes.
5. Now add chicken and optional green chilies. Stir for about 30 seconds so the chicken is mixed well with caramelized onion, ginger, garlic puree.
6. Now add chopped up fresh mint leaves. Mix well. Switch off heat cover and let it sit for 30 seconds to a minute for the mint to wilt. Add additional salt if needed and serve with basmati rice.

Recipe notes:

- This chicken is perfect to add to pizza, burrito, quesadilla, or salads.
- This recipe may be modified to make mint chicken curry. In this case, follow similar steps as in spinach chicken to blend the mint leaves. Add ½ cup water to get enough sauce.
- ½ cup cilantro may also be added to make this a mint-cilantro chicken dish.

My Recipe Notes

Result: Loved it ♥ Okay ☑ Not for me ☒

Spice Level: Too Spicy 😅 Just Right 🙂 Not Spicy Enough 😎

Date(s):

Comments:

EASY SPICY CHICKEN STEW #1

Ingredients
- 1 lbs. chicken breast cut into 1-inch pieces
- 1-2 tsp of curry powder
- 2 jalapenos slit (optional)
- ¼ teaspoon black pepper powder
- 1 medium onion chopped
- 2-3 tsp coconut oil
- 1 16 oz bag of frozen mixed vegetables
- Salt to taste
- ½ -1 can of chicken broth (depending on the amount gravy desired)
- ½ cup cilantro chopped

Method
1. Instant pot set to sauté, heat oil, sauté onions, and optional jalapenos until onions become translucent.
2. Add curry powder and mix for 1-2 minutes so the spices are cooked.
3. Add mixed vegetable and chicken and mix well so chicken and vegetables are coated with the curry powder.
4. Add chicken broth and close lid. Now set to either poultry and cook or manual pressure-cooking set for 10 minutes.
5. Release steam naturally, add black pepper powder, cilantro and salt to taste.

My Recipe Notes

Result: Loved it ♥   Okay ☑   Not for me ☒

Spice Level: Too Spicy 😖   Just Right 🙂   Not Spicy Enough 😎

Date(s):

Comments:

EASY SPICY CHICKEN STEW #2

Ingredients

- 1 lbs. chicken breast cut into 1-inch pieces
- 2 jalapenos slit (optional)
- 1 teaspoon black pepper powder
- 1 teaspoon paprika
- ½ teaspoon turmeric powder
- 2 teaspoon ginger-garlic paste
- 1 medium onion chopped
- 2-3 tsp coconut oil
- 2 medium potatoes peeled and cubed
- 2 stalks of celery cut into ½ inch slices
- 1 large carrot cut into thin slices
- 3 medium tomatoes
- 1-2 cups of chicken/bone broth (depending on the amount gravy desired)
- ½ cup cilantro chopped

Method

1. Heat oil in a large enough pan, sauté onions, jalapenos until onions become translucent, add ginger garlic paste, paprika, turmeric, and black pepper powder. Mix for 1-2 minutes so the spices are cooked.
2. Add all the vegetables and chicken. Add chicken broth and cover and cook for 20-25 minutes or until the vegetables and chicken are cooked.
3. Add cilantro and salt.

My Recipe Notes

Result: Loved it ♥   Okay ☑ Not for me ☒

Spice Level: Too Spicy 😵 Just Right 🙂 Not Spicy Enough 😎

Date(s):

Comments:

EASY SPICY MASALA CHICKEN

Basic Ingredients
- 10 drumsticks skin off
- 2 tablespoon coconut oil (olive oil or vegetable oil can be used as well)
- 1 cup salsa (mild, medium or hot based on your spice level)
- 1 onion chopped
- 1 tsp turmeric powder
- 2-4 tsp coriander powder
- 2 tsp chili powder
- 2 teaspoon lemon juice
- 2-4 teaspoon ginger-garlic paste
- ½ tsp salt or to taste
- ½ cup cilantro copped
- 1-2 cups of chicken broth/water
- 2 spring curry leaves (optional)
- 2 jalapenos finely diced (optional)

Method
1. Make a couple of deep cuts/grooves in each of the drumsticks and marinate using ½ tsp turmeric, 1 tsp chili powder, lemon juice, salt, and ginger-garlic paste and set aside for 15 minutes (or more)
2. Heat oil and sauté onions, optional curry leaves, and jalapenos. Add rest of the spices powders and mix well. cook them for about 30 seconds or until the spices are cooked and fragrant. Now add salsa.
3. Add the chicken pieces and mix well so that chicken pieces are well coated with the spice mix.
4. Add water and mix well and cover and cook for 20-25 minutes or until chicken is cooked and tender.
5. Garnish with cilantro

Serve with rice or bread.

My Recipe Notes

Result: Loved it ♥   Okay ☑ Not for me ☒

Spice Level: Too Spicy 😄 Just Right 🙂 Not Spicy Enough 😎

Date(s):

Comments:

SPICY PICKLED CHICKEN

Indian and South Asian pickles are very spicy unlike the pickles in North America and Europe. The Asian pickle spice mix generally include a generous amount of chili powder, turmeric, mustard seeds, fenugreek seeds, and asafetida. While spicy vegetable pickles are very popular, meat, fish, and shrimp can also be pickled. There are many ways to pickle chicken. The idea is to soak small pieces of marinated and fried chicken in a sauce containing a lot of chili and other ingredients and vinegar. Pickle can last several weeks in the fridge and is consumed in moderation.

Ingredients

- 1-1/2 lbs. boneless chicken breasts cut into ½ inch or smaller cubes
- 4 tablespoon vegetable oil
- 1 cup finely chopped onions
- 2-4 tablespoon red chili powder
- 1 teaspoon turmeric powder
- 2-inch ginger piece finely chopped (or paste)
- 10-12 cloves of garlic chopped (or paste)
- 10 green chilies or jalapeno peppers chopped (optional)
- 2 spring curry leaves
- 1 teaspoon mustard seeds
- 1 teaspoon fenugreek seeds
- ½-1 cup vinegar (white/ red wine / rice wine/apple cider)
- ½ teaspoon salt or to taste

Method

1. Use 1 tablespoon chili powder, ½ teaspoon turmeric, 1 tablespoon vinegar, and salt to mix with the chicken pieces. Marinate for 30 minutes or overnight.
2. Pre-heat oven to 400 degrees and bake the chicken pieces for 10-15 minutes so they get cooked and individual chicken pieces are dry with spices on them and separated from each other.
3. Heat oil, crackle mustard seeds, and fenugreek seeds. sauté onions, garlic, ginger, green chilies, and curry leaves for 1-2minutes. Add rest of the spices and mix for another 1-2 minutes or the spices are cooked.
4. Now add the baked chicken pieces. Mix well.
5. Add vinegar, cover and simmer for 3-4 minutes.
6. Add additional salt if required and mix. Let it cool down.
7. Transfer it into a glass jar and use it as a condiment to add flavor to your dishes or a side dish. It should last in the fridge for at least a month.

Recipe notes:

1. Though vegetable oil is used in the recipe as it is easier to buy, mustard oil is the best oil to make spicy pickles.
2. There are several alternative ways to make this pickle and each may come out a bit different than the recipe given above.
   a. Instead of baking the marinated chicken, it could be fried in oil first before mixing with the pickle masala.
   b. If you are frying chicken in oil, then the easy next step is to add all the rest of the ingredients into the same pan and then follow steps 5-7 above.

3. The same recipe may be tried without marinating in the interest of time and you can get similar results.
4. You could substitute 2-3 tablespoons of lemon juice instead of vinegar.
5. Try the same recipe with different vinegar and see how you like it.
6. Since this dish can be kept for a long time in the fridge and is only used as a side in moderation, care must be taken every time you use a spoon to take pickle, the spoon needs to be dry and clean, or the pickle could go bad.

My Recipe Notes

Result: Loved it ♥   Okay ☑   Not for me ☒

Spice Level: Too Spicy 😊   Just Right ☺   Not Spicy Enough 😎

Date(s):

Comments:

Notes:

KALE AND CHICKEN FRY

Kale is a superfood and kale and chicken a very healthy combination. The simplest way to make this is to make chicken with spices following any one of the recipes above, make kale chips and just crumble the chips into the chicken and mix well.

Ingredients
- 2 lbs. boneless chicken breast cut into 1-inch cubes/strips
- 2 tsp coconut oil (olive oil or vegetable oil can be used as well)
- 1/2 tsp turmeric powder
- 1-2 tsp black pepper powder
- 2 tsp coriander powder
- 2 large onion sliced
- 2-inch piece of ginger thinly sliced
- Salt to taste
- 2-3 medium tomato sliced
- 4-6 cloves of garlic crushed
- Cilantro – 1 cup (optional)
- 2 cups of green or red kale washed and cut/tore into 1-2 inch pieces (to make kale chips)

Method
1. Heat oil in a medium non-stick pan; add onions, garlic and ginger. Stir until golden.
2. Add pepper coriander powder, pepper powder and turmeric, stir for one minute and then add tomato and mix well.
3. Add chicken mix so that chicken is coated well with spices and onion.
4. Cover and simmer for 20-25 minutes or until the chicken is cooked stirring occasionally so the chicken or the gravy does not stick to the pan.
5. Meanwhile in parallel, spread the kale pieces on a cookie sheet and put in the oven at 350 degrees for 10 minutes or the kale become chips and can easily crumble.
6. Once the chicken is cooked, take the kale chips and crumble using your hand and spread it on top of chicken fry.
7. Mix well and cover it for 1 minute. Garnish with cilantro. Serve with rice or naan (Indian bread).

Recipe Note:
1. You can also make chicken and kale using the earlier saag chicken recipe. In this case, you cook/steam kale first and cook chicken the blended kale and spice mix.

My Recipe Notes

Result: Loved it ♥   Okay ☑ Not for me ☒

Spice Level: Too Spicy 😊 Just Right 🙂 Not Spicy Enough 😎

Date(s):

Comments:

BUTTER CHICKEN

Ingredients

- 2lbs. chicken breast cut into 1-inch pieces
- One large finely chopped onion
- ½ teaspoon ginger paste
- ½ teaspoon garlic paste
- ½ teaspoon coriander powder
- ½ teaspoon garam masala powder
- ¼ tsp cayenne pepper
- 1 teaspoon cumin powder
- ¼ cup cashews, soaked in water
- 1 tablespoon coconut or olive oil
- 4 medium tomato chopped

To marinate:

- ½ cup yogurt
- ½ teaspoon turmeric powder
- ½ teaspoon red chili powder
- ½ teaspoon salt
- ½ tsp garam masala powder

Method

1. Make a marinade by mixing yogurt, turmeric powder, and chili powder. In a large enough bowl, apply marinade on the chicken pieces. Mix it well and keep it the fridge at least 2 for hours, preferably overnight.

2. The next step is to bake or fry the marinated chicken. To bake, set the oven to 400 degrees Fahrenheit. Spread the chicken evenly on a baking tray and bake it for about 8-10 minutes just enough to make the chicken tender. Alternatively, add a tablespoon oil in a non-stick pan and fry the chicken pieces for about 5 minutes to make it dry and crispy.

3. Heat oil in a pan on medium heat. Add chopped onions and sauté for a few minutes or until onions become translucent. Add the ginger-garlic paste, coriander powder, black pepper powder, and cumin powder. Mix well for a minute and then add chopped tomatoes and cashews. Let it cook it for 2-3 minutes or until the oil starts to separate. Switch off the heat and let it cool down.

4. Grind the saluted mix from step 3 and set aside.

5. Melt the button in the saucepan and pour the blended puree back into the pan. Bring it to a boil and cook for 5 minutes or until the gravy thickens.

6. Add baked/fried chicken. Cook covered for another 5-10 minutes or until chicken is cooked and tender.

7. Add salt to taste. Garnish with cilantro and serve.

Recipe Notes:
1. If you like more creamy and rich butter chicken, add 1/3 cup of whipping cream, heavy cream or coconut milk after step 6 and mix well.
2. Optionally you can add some dried fenugreek leaves (methi) in step 5. This gives a distinct flavor.
3. Tandoori masala may be used instead of garam masala for marination.
4. Vegan options: Substitute chicken with tofu, mushrooms, potato or cauliflower

My Recipe Notes

Result: Loved it ♥   Okay ☑   Not for me ☒

Spice Level: Too Spicy 😖   Just Right 😊   Not Spicy Enough 😎

Date(s):

Comments:

Notes:

COCONUT CHICKEN CURRY RICE

Coconut has many health benefits including antioxidant and anti-inflammatory benefits. A spicy coconut chicken curry is a dish as healthy as it gets.

Ingredients

- 1 cups basmati rice washed
- 1.5 cup frozen peas + chopped carrots
- 1 can of 15 oz coconut milk
- 2 tbsp olive oil
- 1 bay leaf
- 2-3 crushed cardamoms
- 2-3 cloves
- 2 tsp ginger garlic paste
- 1 lb. chicken (drumsticks or thighs)
- 2 tbsp grated coconut (optional)
- 2 tsp curry powder
- Salt to taste
- 1 cup water/chicken or bone broth

Method

1. Set instant pot to sauté. Add oil and toast cardamoms, cloves, bay leaf, ginger-garlic paste, and optional grated coconut for 30 seconds.
2. Now add curry powder and mix well. Sauté for a minute or until the curry powder is fragrant. Add vegetables and chicken. Mix well and cook for 10 minutes or until vegetables are softened and chicken is coated with spices. Add coconut milk, water, and salt. Mix. Stir in rice. Close and cook on white rice setting with valve in sealing position.
3. Once the rice is cooked and steam is released naturally, open the lid and serve.

My Recipe Notes

Result: Loved it ♥   Okay ☑   Not for me ☒

Spice Level: Too Spicy 😎   Just Right 🙂   Not Spicy Enough 😎

Date(s):

Comments:

SPICY CHICKEN AND MANGO RECIPE IDEA #1

Mango chicken curry offers a blast of tangy, sweet, and spicy flavors. There are a couple of recipe ideas below. Also, you could try many variations following some of the ideas listed in the recipe notes.

Ingredients

- 2 lbs. boneless chicken breast cut into 1-inch cubes
- 2 tablespoon coconut oil (olive oil or vegetable oil can be used as well)
- 1 medium red onion chopped
- 1 ripe mango peeled and sliced
- 1 red bell pepper thinly sliced
- 2 teaspoon curry powder
- 2-inch ginger peeled and grated or finely chopped
- 3-4 cloves of garlic peeled and crushed
- ½ tsp salt or to taste
- 2 springs curry leaves/ ¼ cup coriander leaves
- 1 can (14/16 oz) coconut milk
- ½ cup chicken broth/water

Method

1. Heat oil and sauté onions, (optional) curry leaves, ginger, and garlic. Add curry powder and cook them for about 1-2 minutes or until the spices are cooked and fragrant.
2. Add bell pepper and mango pieces. Mix well. Add chicken broth/water and salt. Bring to a boil on medium heat.
3. Add the chicken pieces and mix well so that chicken pieces are well coated with the spice mix. Cover and cook for about 10-15 minutes or until chicken is cooked through.
4. Add coconut milk and simmer for 3-4 minutes.
5. Garnish with cilantro (optional)

My Recipe Notes

Result: Loved it ♥   Okay ☑ Not for me ☒

Spice Level: Too Spicy 😊 Just Right 🙂 Not Spicy Enough 😎

Date(s):

Comments:

SPICY CHICKEN AND MANGO RECIPE IDEA #2

Ingredients
- 6 chicken thighs skinned and washed
- 3 tablespoon coconut oil (olive oil or vegetable oil can be used as well)
- 2 medium red onions chopped
- 1 ripe mango peeled and sliced
- 1 red bell pepper thinly sliced
- ½-1 tsp turmeric powder
- 1 tsp chili powder
- 1 tsp coriander powder
- ½ tsp cumin seeds
- ½ tsp fresh peppercorns
- 2-inch ginger peeled and grated or finely chopped
- 3-4 cloves of garlic peeled and crushed
- ½ tsp salt or to taste
- 1 tsp lemon juice
- 2 springs curry leaves/ ¼ cup coriander leaves
- 1 can (14/16 oz) coconut milk
- ½ cup chicken broth/water

Method
1. Sprinkle ¼ tsp turmeric, ½ tsp chili powder and ½ tsp salt on chicken thighs along with lemon juice and mix well and set aside for 15 minutes.
2. Heat 1 tablespoon oil and sauté onions, (optional) curry leaves, ginger, and garlic. Add all the spices and cook them for about 1-2 minutes or until the spices are cooked and fragrant. Now add the mango pieces and mix well. Let it cool and blend the mix to make a puree and set it aside.
3. Heat rest of the oil and fry the chicken thighs until all sides are slightly cooked (2-3 minutes) Add bell pepper and mix well.
4. Add the mango-spice puree, chicken broth/water, and salt. Cover and cook for about 8-10 minutes or until chicken is cooked through.
5. Add coconut milk and simmer for 3-4 minutes.
6. Garnish with cilantro (optional)

Mango chicken recipe notes:

1. You can substitute curry powder (in recipe idea #1) or different spices with 2 teaspoons of curry paste, Thai red curry paste or garam masala.
2. Instead of coconut milk, you can use heavy cream.
3. You can add ½ cup non-fat Greek (or regular) yogurt to the marinade instead of lime juice.
4. Try adding 1 tablespoon soy sauce.
5. You can try all these variations with either cut mango pieces or pureed mango.
6. Depending on how ripe the mango is, the sweet-sour balance will change.
7. Try different herbs to garnish instead of cilantro – mint, basil, or lemongrass.

My Recipe Notes

Result: Loved it ♥   Okay ☑   Not for me ☒

Spice Level: Too Spicy 😊   Just Right 🙂   Not Spicy Enough 😎

Date(s):

Comments:

CHICKEN AND VEGETABLE STEW IN COCONUT MILK

Ingredients

- ½ lb. chicken breast cubed
- 1-inch fresh ginger grated or thinly sliced
- 2-3 cloves of garlic crushed
- 1 medium carrot cut into ½ inch pieces
- 1 large potato and cut into cubes
- ¼ head of cauliflower cut into pieces
- ½ cup green peas
- ½ cup green beans cut into 1-inch pieces
- Salt to taste
- 3 cups of coconut milk
- 1 tbsp lime juice
- ¼ cup cilantro or curry leaves chopped
- 1 tsp mustard seeds
- 6 green chilies/jalapenos slit
- 2 tsp black pepper
- 1 spring curry leaves
- 1-inch cinnamon stick
- 1 pinch garam masala or curry powder
- 2 star anise
- 2 bay leaves
- 2 tablespoon coconut oil

Method

1. Heat oil in a pan, fry the mustard seeds, bay leaves, cinnamon, and star anise and curry leaves.

2. Add onions, green chilies, ginger, garlic stir until onions become translucent. Add pepper and garam masala and stir.

3. Add chopped vegetables and chicken and mix well until vegetables and vegetables and chicken are covered with the spices. Cover and cook for about 5 minutes on low-medium, stirring occasionally so the ingredients do not stick to the bottom. There should be enough water from chicken and vegetables to cook for about 5 minutes.

4. Add the coconut milk. Cover and simmer for another 10 minutes or until chicken is cooked and vegetables are tender.

Add salt and enjoy.

My Recipe Notes

Result: Loved it ♥   Okay ☑   Not for me ☒

Spice Level: Too Spicy 😎   Just Right 😊   Not Spicy Enough 😎

Date(s):

Comments:

GINGER CHICKEN MASALA

This curry recipe is inspired by North Indian chicken curry recipes. It contains spices and herbs, and ginger is a key ingredient. This dish is served with rice or Indian bread.

Ingredients

- 8 pieces of chicken legs – 4 thighs and 4 drumsticks
- 1 tsp red chili powder
- 1/2 tsp turmeric
- 2 medium onion chopped
- 2-3 tsp coconut oil
- 2 tsp black pepper
- 4-6 tsp ginger paste, finely grated ginger
- 1 spring curry leaves
- 1 tsp fennel seeds
- 2 tsp cumin seeds
- ½ cup grated coconut
- 1 tsp lime juice
- Salt to taste

Method

1. In a spice blender, grind coconut, black pepper, cumin seeds, and fennel seeds. Add a bit of water and grind it into a smooth paste.

2. Add oil in a pan and sauté onions become translucent. Add ginger and curry leaves and mix well until the curry leaves are fried and fragrant. Add chili powder and salt. Mix well.

3. Add chicken and masala paste and mix well until the chicken pieces are well coated with the masala. Add two cups of water. Cover and cook on low flame until chicken is done. Garnish with chopped cilantro (optional)

Serve with rice or bread.

My Recipe Notes

Result: Loved it ♥   Okay ☑   Not for me ☒

Spice Level: Too Spicy 😎   Just Right 🙂   Not Spicy Enough 😎

Date(s):

Comments:

_____

_____

_____

_____

_____

_____

_____

_____

_____

_____

_____

_____

_____

_____

_____

_____

_____

SPICY GARLIC CHICKEN

Ingredients

- 1-1/2 lbs. chicken breast cut into 1-inch pieces
- 20 cloves of garlic – each crushed
- 1/2 tsp turmeric
- 2 tablespoon Kashmiri chili powder
- 1-2 teaspoon garam masala/curry powder
- 1 tsp ginger-garlic paste
- 1 red onion chopped
- 4 tomatoes chopped
- 3-4 tsp oil
- ½ tsp pepper powder
- Salt to taste
- ½ -1 can of chicken broth/water (depending on the amount gravy desired)

Method

1. Marinate chicken with all the spices, ginger garlic paste, salt, and yogurt. Mix well and keep it aside for 10 minutes (or overnight)
2. Make a puree of onions and tomatoes.
3. Heat oil and roast crushed garlic cloves for about 30 seconds. Add marinated chicken and mix well so the chicken gets cooked outside with all the spices for about 1-2 minutes.
4. Now add the tomato-onion puree, bring it to a boil
5. Add enough broth/water for the desired amount of gravy. Cover and cook until chicken is cooked.

Serve with rice or bread.

Recipe notes:

1. You will be able to bite cloves of roasted garlic in the finished recipe. This is on purpose.
2. If you prefer the strong garlicky flavor but do not want to bite roasted garlic cloves, after roasting, garlic may also be pureed along with tomato and onions. In this case, first roast garlic and then do step 2.
3. Like many other recipes, this recipe is also easily adapted instant pot which will save much time. If using instant pot use sauté function first and then cook in manual or poultry setting.
4. You can use cilantro, curry leaves or basil leaves to garnish.

My Recipe Notes

Result: Loved it ♥   Okay ☑   Not for me ☒

Spice Level: Too Spicy 😎   Just Right ☺   Not Spicy Enough 😎

Date(s):

Comments:

CHICKEN TIKKA MASALA

Ingredients
- 2lbs. chicken breast cut into 1-inch pieces

To marinate:
- 1 cup yogurt
- ½- 1 teaspoon turmeric powder
- ½ -1 teaspoon chili powder
- ½ teaspoon salt
- ½ teaspoon ginger paste
- 1 teaspoon garlic paste
- ½ - 1 teaspoon garam masala

For the sauce
- One large finely chopped onion
- ½ -1 teaspoon ginger finely grated
- ½ -1 teaspoon garlic finely chopped
- 1 teaspoon coriander powder
- ½ - 1 teaspoon garam masala powder
- ½ - 1 teaspoon cayenne pepper or Kashmiri chili powder
- ½ -2 teaspoon chili powder (optional, if you like spicier)
- 1 teaspoon cumin powder
- 1 – 2 teaspoon turmeric powder
- 3 tablespoon coconut or olive oil
- 3 cups of tomato sauce
- 1 cup heavy cream
- 1 cup water
- 1 teaspoon brown sugar (optional)
- ¼ cup cilantro chopped

Method

1. Combine chicken with all of the ingredients for the chicken marinade; Mix well and let the chicken marinate for 30 minutes or overnight if you prefer.
2. Fry or bake the marinated chicken.
   - If you are frying, heat oil in a large pan. Add chicken pieces in batches. Fry until browned on all sides and set aside. 2-3 minutes in oil should fry them sufficiently.

    o If you are baking, pre-heat oven to 450 degrees (F), bake them on a skewer in a baking pan. Bake for about 15-20 minutes or chicken becomes slightly dark brown outside.

3. Fry the onions in oil. If you had fried chicken in the previous step, the same pan and oil may be used to fry onions. If you baked, add oil and fry onions in a large pan.
4. Add garlic and ginger and sauté for 1 minute, then add garam masala, cumin, turmeric, and coriander. Fry for about 10-20 seconds until fragrant. Make sure the spices do not burn.
5. Pour in the tomato puree, chili powders and salt. Add fried or baked chicken along with any juices from frying/baking. Simmer for about 10-15 minutes on low heat, stir occasionally until the sauce become thick with a deep brown-red color.
6. Stir in the cream and optional sugar. Cook for an additional 5 minutes or until chicken is cooked well. Add water if the sauce becomes too thick.
7. Garnish with cilantro and serve with basmati rice.

Recipe Notes:

1. Depending on your tolerance level, you can adjust the amount of spices used in this recipe.
2. The recipe is healthier than the restaurant bought tikka masala as restaurants usually use red food color to color the chicken.
3. Tandoori masala may be used instead of garam masala for marinating.
4. Chili powder may be completely replaced with cayenne powder or Kashmiri chili powder. Both are milder and imparts better color to the sauce than regular chili powder.

My Recipe Notes

Result: Loved it ♥   Okay ☑   Not for me ☒

Spice Level: Too Spicy 😵   Just Right 🙂   Not Spicy Enough 😎

Date(s):

Comments:

_____

_____

_____

_____

_____

_____

_____

_____

_____

_____

_____

_____

_____

_____

_____

_____

Notes:

EASY CHICKEN CURRY WITH TOMATOES

The next several recipes are simple recipes for making chicken curry. I am following an eighty-twenty rule for these recipes under the "Easy" heading. The idea is to make 100% healthy dishes using ingredients (such as spices and herbs) that have been proven over the years to have immense health benefits and retain at least 80% yumminess of the original dish BUT with only 20% of the effort.

Ingredients

- 2 lbs. chicken breast cut into small (1 inch) pieces
- 1-2 tsp of curry powder
- 1/2 tsp turmeric
- 2 medium onion chopped
- 2-3 tsp coconut oil
- ½ tsp pepper powder
- 2 tbsp ginger garlic paste (or 1 tbsp ginger paste and 1 tbsp garlic paste)
- 1 spring of curry leaves
- 2 medium tomatoes, chopped
- 1 tsp lime juice

Method

1. Heat oil in a large enough pan and sauté onions, garlic and ginger until onions become translucent.
2. Add curry powder, pepper powder, coriander, and cumin and mix for 1-2 minutes so the spices are cooked. Make sure not to burn spices.
3. Add chicken and mix it on high heat for one minute so that any raw spices sticking to the chicken as the marinade get fried in oil and the chicken pieces are well coated with spices and herbs. Add tomatoes, cover and cook for 15-20 minutes on low heat. No need to add water. The moisture in the chicken and tomatoes are enough. Stir occasionally.
4. Once the chicken is cooked, add cilantro and stir. Add salt to taste. Switch of the heat and keep it covered for a 1-2 minutes before serving.

Serve with rice or bread.

My Recipe Notes

Result: Loved it ♥   Okay ☑   Not for me ☒

Spice Level: Too Spicy 😅   Just Right 🙂   Not Spicy Enough 😎

Date(s):

Comments:

EASY CHICKEN CURRY WITH COCONUT MILK

Ingredients

- 2 lbs. chicken thighs and legs, bone-in
- 1-2 tsp of curry powder, depending on your tolerance to spice
- 2 tbsp coriander powder
- 2 medium onions, chopped
- 2-3 tsp coconut oil
- 1 tsp pepper powder
- ½ tsp cumin powder
- 2 tbsp ginger garlic paste (or 1 tbsp ginger paste and 1 tbsp garlic paste)
- 1 can coconut milk
- ¼ teaspoon salt
- 1 tsp lime juice
- 2 springs of curry leaves

Method

1. Sprinkle ½ tsp curry powder, turmeric, lime juice, and ¼ tsp salt on cut chicken. Mix well and keep aside for 30 minutes.
2. In a separate pan, heat oil and add curry leaves and immediately add onions, and ginger and sauté until onions become translucent. Be careful when curry leaves are added, as it may splatter hot oil.
3. Add remaining curry powder, pepper powder, coriander, and cumin and mix for 1-2 minutes so the spices are cooked. Make sure not to burn spices.
4. Add chicken and mix it on high heat for one minute so that any raw spices sticking to the chicken as marinade gets fried in oil and also the chicken pieces are well coated with spices and herbs. Add tomato, cover and cook for 15-20 minutes on low flame. There is no need to add water, the moisture in chicken and tomato is enough. Stir occasionally.
5. Once the chicken is cooked, add coconut milk and stir well. Add salt to taste. Switch off the heat and keep it covered for 1-2 minutes before serving.

Serve with rice or bread.

My Recipe Notes

Result: Loved it ♥   Okay ☑   Not for me ☒

Spice Level: Too Spicy 😖   Just Right 🙂   Not Spicy Enough 😎

Date(s):

Comments:

EASY CHICKEN CURRY WITH POTATOES

This recipe is another simplified chicken curry recipe. By now, you may have noticed that you can make a number of simple or easy chicken curries by altering the ingredients in the curry slightly. You can apply your creativity to vary the amount of spices or the spice/herb combinations and even the cooking medium (coconut/vegetable/olive/butter) and get delicious and different curry results.

Ingredients

- 2 lbs. chicken thighs and legs bone-in
- 1-2 tsp of mild curry powder, depending on your tolerance on spice
- 2 tbsp coriander powder
- ½ tsp turmeric powder
- 2 medium onion chopped
- 2-3 tsp coconut oil
- ½ tsp garam masala
- ½ tsp cumin powder
- 2 tbsp ginger garlic paste (or 1 tbsp ginger paste and 1 tbsp garlic paste)
- 2 medium potatoes peeled and cut
- 2-3 medium tomatoes sliced
- Salt to taste
- ½ -1 can of chicken broth (depending on the amount gravy desired)
- ½ cup cilantro chopped

Method

1. Sprinkle ½ tsp curry powder, turmeric, and ¼ tsp salt on cut chicken. Mix well and keep it aside for 30 minutes.
2. In a separate pan, heat oil, sauté onions, garlic, curry leaves, and ginger until onions become translucent.
3. Add remaining curry powder, and also the other spices and mix for 1-2 minutes so the spices are cooked. Make sure not to burn spices.
4. Add potatoes, mix well and cook covered for 5 minutes or until potatoes are tender. Now add chicken and mix it on high heat for one minute so that any raw spices sticking to the chicken as marinade gets fried in oil and also the chicken pieces are well coated with spices and herbs. Add tomato, cover, and cook for 15-20 minutes on low flame. Add enough chicken broth for the desired thickness. Stir occasionally.
5. Once the chicken and potatoes are cooked, add cilantro and stir. Add salt to taste. Switch off the heat and keep it covered for about 1-2 minutes before serving.

Serve with rice or bread.

My Recipe Notes

Result: Loved it ♥   Okay ☑   Not for me ☒

Spice Level: Too Spicy 😖   Just Right 🙂   Not Spicy Enough 😎

Date(s):

Comments:

EASY CHICKEN CURRY IN INSTANT POT

The easy chicken curry recipes described above can be quickly made in an instant pot. If you are using an instant pot, these dishes could be made in 20 minutes or less. The simple sequence will be to use the sauté function in most instant pots to sauté the onions and spices and then add chicken and (optional) vegetables and then add the liquid you want the chicken to cook in (broth, water or coconut milk), close the lid and cook for 5-10 minutes in high pressure or simply select poultry from the function selector on the instant pot. Cooking cannot get easier than this.

Ingredients

- 2 lbs. chicken the way you like (bone-in thighs or drumsticks or bone-out cut to pieces)
- 1-2 tsp of mild curry powder, depending on your tolerance on spice
- 2 tbsp coriander powder
- ½ tsp turmeric powder
- 2 medium onion chopped
- 2-3 tsp coconut oil
- ½ tsp garam masala
- ½ tsp cumin powder
- 2 tbsp ginger garlic paste (or 1 tbsp ginger paste and 1 tbsp garlic paste)
- 2 medium potatoes peeled and cut (optional #1)
- 2-3 medium tomatoes sliced (optional #2)
- 2-3 Italian squash sliced into thick (1/2 inch) slices (optional #3)
- 2 Bell pepper sliced (optional #4)
- Salt to taste
- ½ -1 can of chicken broth (depending on the amount gravy desired)
- ½ cup cilantro chopped

Method

1. Instant pot set to sauté, heat oil, sauté onions, garlic, curry leaves, and ginger until onions become translucent.
2. Add curry powder, and also the other spices and mix for 1-2 minutes so the spices are cooked. Make sure not to burn spices.
3. Add chicken and any one or more of the optional vegetables. Mix well.
4. Add chicken broth and close lid. Now set to either poultry and cook or manual pressure-cooking set for 10 minutes.

Serve with rice or bread.

My Recipe Notes

Result: Loved it ♥   Okay ☑   Not for me ☒

Spice Level: Too Spicy 😅   Just Right 🙂   Not Spicy Enough 😎

Date(s):

Comments:

EASY CHICKEN BIRIYANI

This is one of the easiest and quickest ways to make biriyani or chicken spiced rice. It uses rotisserie chicken that cuts down cooking time at least by half.

Ingredients:

- ½ of a rotisserie chicken - skin off. cut into pieces. Bone in/removed based on preference
- 1 cup cilantro chopped
- 1 cup mint leaves chopped
- 1 medium onion – sliced
- 3 tsp. butter
- 2-3 tomatoes sliced
- 2-3 teaspoons of biriyani powder (you can get biriyani powder online or from south Asian stores)
- 2 cups basmati rice

Method:

1. Cook the rice in a rice cooker. For biriyani, you want the rice to be not fully cooked and individual grains should remain separate. One way to do this is to reduce the amount of water. Put 3/4 of usual amount of water. In this case, about 2-1/2 to 3 cups of water. Add 1 tsp butter and optionally 2-3 cardamom pods/ 2-3 cloves crushed while cooking rice (not listed in ingredients - completely optional)
2. In parallel, while the rice is cooking, sauté onion in an instant pot/pressure cooker. Add 2-3 teaspoon biriyani masala and mix well so masala gets cooked (but not burnt). Add tomatoes and mix. Add half of cilantro and mint. Mix. Now add the cooked rotisserie chicken and mix well.
3. By this time, the rice should be cooked. spread this rice in two layers on top of the chicken with herbs separating them.
4. Close the instant pot and cook the rice (rice cook setting) for about 5 minutes.
5. Open after about 10-15 minutes or when the pressure is reduced.

Recipe Notes:
1. You can use fresh chicken instead of rotisserie chicken to make biriyani. In this case, marinate the chicken in yogurt and spices first. Then follow the steps above but cook chicken for 5 minutes before layering rice and herbs.

My Recipe Notes

Result: Loved it ♥   Okay ☑   Not for me ☒

Spice Level: Too Spicy 😖   Just Right ☺   Not Spicy Enough 😎

Date(s):

Comments:

EASY CHICKEN CURRY WITH GREEN PLANTAIN

Raw plantain can be curried as stand-alone or combined with meat dishes. This recipe uses roasted curry powder. You can buy roasted curry powder from local south Asian or online stores.

Ingredients

- 1 lb. chicken – anyway you like it
- 2 tsp of roasted curry powder
- 1 medium onion chopped
- ½ tsp turmeric powder
- ½ - 1tsp garam masala powder (optional)
- 2-3 tsp coconut oil
- 2 tsp ginger garlic paste
- 1 green plantain washed, edges removed and cut into 1-inch cubes, skin on.
- Salt to taste
- ½ -1 can of chicken broth (depending on the amount gravy desired)
- 2 tomatoes chopped (optional)
- 2 Jalapenos slit (optional)
- 1 spring curry leaves (optional)

Method

1. In a large enough pan, heat oil, sauté onions, ginger garlic paste, jalapenos, and curry leaves until onions become translucent.
2. Add all the spices and mix for 1-2 minutes so the spices are cooked.
3. Add plantain and chicken and mix so the chicken pieces are well coated with spices. Add tomato and enough chicken broth for the desired thickness. Mix well and cook covered for 15-20 minutes.
4. Once the chicken and plantain are cooked, add salt to taste. Switch off the heat and keep it covered for a 1-2 minutes before serving.

Serve with rice or bread.

Recipe Notes:

1. You can try the recipe with unroasted curry powder and see how you like it.
2. If roasted curry powder is not available, the simplest way to make roasted curry powder is by roasting red chilies, coriander seeds, cumin seeds, black peppercorns, and fennel seeds and then grinding in a spice grinder.

My Recipe Notes

Result: Loved it ♥   Okay ☑ Not for me ☒

Spice Level: Too Spicy 😎 Just Right ☺ Not Spicy Enough 😎

Date(s):

Comments:

BELL PEPPER AND CHICKEN STIR FRY

Basic Ingredients

- 1 bell pepper washed and cut into thin slices (use the different color peppers as you desire)
- 2 tsp coconut oil (olive oil or vegetable oil can be used as well)
- 1 lb. boneless chicken breast cut into thin strips
- 1 tsp turmeric powder
- 1 tsp black pepper powder
- 1 tsp coriander powder
- 1 medium onion sliced
- ½ inch piece of ginger thinly sliced
- Salt to taste
- 1-2 medium tomato sliced
- 3 cloves of garlic crushed

Optional Ingredients

- 1 Jalapeño pepper sliced into thin pieces
- ¼ cup cilantro chopped

Method

1. Sprinkle ½ spoons of turmeric powder, pepper powder and salt on the washed and cut chicken, mix well and set aside for 10 minutes.
2. In a pan, heat oil, add onions, crushed garlic, ginger and optional Jalapeno. Sauté till onions become translucent.
3. Add rest of turmeric powder, coriander powder and pepper powder and mix well.
4. Add tomato and mix.
5. Now add the bell pepper and chicken and mix well.
6. Cover and cook for 10-15 minutes on medium heat or until chicken and peppers are cooked. Stir occasionally.
7. Switch off the heat, add optional cilantro, add more salt if required depending on your taste.

Serve with rice or bread.

My Recipe Notes

Result: Loved it ♥   Okay ☑   Not for me ☒

Spice Level: Too Spicy 😆   Just Right ☺   Not Spicy Enough 😎

Date(s):

Comments:

CHICKEN PEPPER FRY

Ingredients
- 2 lbs. boneless chicken breast cut into 1-inch cubes/strips
- 2 tsp coconut oil (olive oil or vegetable oil can be used as well)
- 1/2 tsp turmeric powder
- 1-2 tsp black pepper powder
- 2 tsp coriander powder
- 2 large onion sliced
- 2-inch piece of ginger thinly sliced
- Salt
- 2-3 medium tomato sliced
- 4-6 cloves of garlic crushed
- Cilantro – 1 cup (optional)

Method
1. Heat oil in a medium non-stick pan; add onions, garlic, and ginger. Stir until golden.
2. Add coriander powder, pepper powder, and turmeric. Stir for 2-3 minutes.
3. Add tomato and mix well.
4. Add chicken and mix so that chicken is coated well with spices and onion.
5. Cover and simmer for 20-25 minutes or until the chicken is cooked stirring occasionally so the chicken or the gravy does not stick to the pan.

Garnish with cilantro. Serve with rice or naan (Indian bread).

My Recipe Notes

Result: Loved it ♥   Okay ☑   Not for me ☒

Spice Level: Too Spicy 😆   Just Right 🙂   Not Spicy Enough 😎

Date(s):

Comments:

_____

_____

_____

_____

_____

_____

_____

_____

_____

_____

_____

_____

_____

_____

_____

CHAPTER 4. MEXICAN INSPIRED SPICY CHICKEN RECIPES

The next several recipes are Mexican inspired dishes that are spicier and simpler to make than their authentic preparations.

SPICED CHICKEN BURRITOS - RECIPE #1

This is an easy recipe for making spicy chicken burritos using either leftover chicken dish (such as tandoori chicken, baked chicken, etc.) or rotisserie chicken.

Ingredients

- 1 cup cooked chicken meat
- 4 tortillas
- ½ inch grated ginger (optional)
- 2 cloves of garlic chopped (optional)
- 1 tsp garam masala or curry powder
- ½ tsp turmeric powder
- 1 jalapeno chopped (optional)
- ½ cup medium salsa
- ¼ cup cilantro
- 1 tsp olive oil
- Salt to taste
- 2 springs of green onions chopped
- ½ cup parmesan cheese

Method

1. Heat oil in a medium pan over medium heat, sauté ginger, garlic and green onions
2. Add turmeric and garam masala/curry powder. Sauté for about a minute until spices become fragrant.
3. Now add cooked chicken and mix well so the chicken is coated with the spices.
4. Add salsa and mix well.
5. Use a flat surface to lay tortillas and divide the spicy chicken filling among 6 tortillas. Top with cheese and cilantro and fold them burrito style.

My Recipe Notes

Result: Loved it ♥   Okay ☑   Not for me ☒

Spice Level: Too Spicy 😅   Just Right 😊   Not Spicy Enough 😎

Date(s):

Comments:

SPICED CHICKEN BURRITOS - RECIPE #2

This recipe uses ground chicken instead of cooked meat from a rotisserie chicken.
Ingredients

- 1 lb. ground chicken
- 4 tortillas
- ½ inch grated ginger (optional)
- 2 cloves of garlic chopped (optional)
- 1 tsp garam masala or curry powder
- ½ tsp turmeric powder
- 1 jalapeno chopped (optional)
- ½ cup medium salsa
- ¼ cup cilantro
- 1 tsp olive oil
- Salt to taste
- 2 springs of green onions chopped
- ½ cup parmesan cheese

Method

1. Heat oil in a medium pan over medium heat, sauté ginger, garlic and green onions
2. Add turmeric and garam masala/curry powder. Sauté for about a minute until spices become fragrant.
3. Now add chicken and mix well so the chicken is coated with the spices.
4. Add salsa. Mix and cook covered for 15 minutes or the chicken is cooked and is mixed well with the spices.
5. Use a flat surface to lay tortillas and divide the spicy chicken filling among 6 tortillas. Top with cheese and cilantro and fold them burrito style.

My Recipe Notes

Result: Loved it ♥   Okay ☑   Not for me ☒

Spice Level: Too Spicy 😅   Just Right 🙂   Not Spicy Enough 😎

Date(s):

Comments:

_____

_____

_____

_____

_____

_____

_____

_____

_____

_____

_____

_____

_____

_____

_____

_____

_____

SPICED CHICKEN QUESADILLA- RECIPE #1

My daughter loves this recipe. This is quick and easy to make.
Ingredients

- 1 cup cooked chicken meat shredded or cut into small cubes (I use meat from a rotisserie chicken)
- 6 tortillas (10-inch size)
- 1 tsp garam masala or curry powder
- ½ tsp grated ginger (optional)
- 2 cloves garlic chopped (optional)
- ½ tsp turmeric powder (optional)
- 1 jalapeno chopped (optional)
- ½ onion chopped
- ¼ cup cilantro
- 1 tsp olive oil
- Salt to taste
- 2 springs of green onions chopped (optional)
- ½ cup mild cheddar cheese

Method

1. Heat oil in a medium pan, sauté onion and one or more of the optional ingredients (except turmeric) as per your taste
2. Add garam masala/curry powder and optional turmeric. Sauté for about 30 seconds.
3. Now add cooked chicken and mix well so the chicken is coated with the spices. Add cilantro.
4. Use a flat surface to lay tortillas. Spread cheese on the tortillas. Divide the spicy chicken filling one side of 6 tortillas.
5. Heat a flat pan and transfer each tortilla carefully into the pan. Once the cheese starts melting, fold it and press with a flat spoon so the edges are sealed with melted cheese.
6. Turn them over and heat it for 15-30 seconds and remove. Repeat this process for the remaining tortillas. Your quesadilla is ready and each one cut into three pieces and serve.

Recipe Notes:

1. Instead of following step 4 above, you could lay each tortilla's in the heated pan and then spread cheese and fillings. This avoids the tricky transfer of a layered tortilla.
2. You may use the oven to back the filled tortillas. In this case, pre-heat the oven to 350 degrees and lay the tortillas all on a cooking sheet. Bake for 10 minutes or until cheese melted. Open oven use a flat spoon to fold and press the tortillas to make a quesadilla.

My Recipe Notes

Result: Loved it ♥   Okay ☑   Not for me ☒

Spice Level: Too Spicy 😆   Just Right 🙂   Not Spicy Enough 😎

Date(s):

Comments:

SPICED CHICKEN QUESADILLA- RECIPE #2

This recipe is a bit more elaborate and uses fresh chicken.

Ingredients

- 1 chicken breast chopped into small pieces
- 6 tortillas (10-inch size)
- ½ tsp chili powder
- ¼ tsp turmeric powder
- ½ tsp garam masala or curry powder
- ½ tsp grated ginger (optional)
- 2 cloves garlic chopped (optional)
- ½ onion chopped
- ½ red bell pepper chopped
- ½ green bell pepper chopped
- ¼ cup cilantro
- 1 tbsp olive oil
- 2 tsp lemon juice
- Salt to taste
- ½ cup mild cheddar cheese

Method

1. Sprinkle the spice powders (turmeric, chili, garam masala powder) on chicken. Add lemon juice and mix well. Refrigerate to marinate for 15 minutes (or more)
2. Heat oil in a medium pan, sauté onion, and all of the optional ingredients.
3. Add chicken and mix well. Cook for 3-5 minutes or until chicken is cooked on medium heat stirring as needed.
4. Now add bell pepper pieces and cook for another 3-4 minutes. Add salt and cilantro and mix well.
5. Use a flat surface to lay tortillas. Spread cheese on the tortillas. Divide the spicy chicken filling one side of 6 tortillas.
6. Heat a flat pan and transfer each tortilla carefully into the pan. Once the cheese starts melting, fold it and press with a flat spoon so the edges are sealed with melted cheese.
7. Turn them over and heat it for 15-30 seconds and remove. Repeat this process for the remaining tortillas. Your quesadilla is ready and each one cut into three pieces and serve.

Recipe Notes:

- Instead of following step 4 above, you could lay each tortilla's in the heated pan and then spread cheese and fillings. This avoids the tricky transfer of a layered tortilla.
- You may use the oven to back the filled tortillas. In this case, pre-heat the oven to 350 degrees and lay the tortillas all on a cooking sheet. Bake for 10 minutes or until cheese melted. Open oven, use a flat spoon to fold and press the tortillas to make a quesadilla.
- The marinated chicken may be backed at 400 degrees for about 10 minutes (or until cooked) and then mix with bell pepper. In this case, skip step 3 in the cooking process and add baked at the end of step 4.

My Recipe Notes

Result: Loved it ♥   Okay ☑   Not for me ☒

Spice Level: Too Spicy 😵   Just Right ☺   Not Spicy Enough 😎

Date(s):

Comments:

_____

_____

_____

_____

_____

_____

_____

_____

_____

_____

_____

_____

_____

_____

_____

EASY SPICED CHICKEN ENCHILADA

This recipe uses meat from a rotisserie chicken for the cooked chicken meat to make a quick and easy spicy enchilada.

Ingredients

- 1 lb. cooked chicken meat shredded
- 10 corn tortillas
- 1 tsp garam masala or curry powder
- ½ tsp grated ginger (optional)
- 2 cloves garlic chopped (optional)
- ½ tsp turmeric powder (optional)
- 1 tsp coriander powder
- 1 tsp cumin powder
- ½ tsp cinnamon powder
- 1 tsp black pepper powder
- 1 jalapeno chopped (optional)
- 1 onion chopped
- 2 cups of tomato sauce
- ¼ cup cilantro
- 1 tsp olive oil
- Salt to taste
- 2 springs of green onions chopped (optional)
- ½ Monterey jack cheese
- ½ cup cheddar cheese
- 2 cups chicken stock/bone broth or water
- 2 tbsp olive oil

Method

1. Heat oil in a medium pan, sauté onion, ginger, garlic and all the rest of the spices. Add tomato sauce and chicken stock. Cook for about 2 minutes. Blend the ingredients into a smooth sauce.
2. Now combine the shredded chicken, green onions, ½ of the cheeses and cilantro, optional jalapenos, and a cup of the sauce from step 1 and mix well.
3. Wrap the corn tortillas in a paper towel or a damp cloth and microwave 15 seconds so it becomes pliable and not break.
4. Grease a 9X13 inch pan with oil, spoon about 1/3 cup of chicken mixture into a corn tortilla and gently roll the tortilla and place it in the baking dish with seam side down. Repeat this for all of the 10 tortillas and place them in the baking dish.
5. Pour the remaining enchilada sauce evenly over the tortillas. Spread the remaining cheese and cilantro on top.
6. Bake at 400 degrees for about 8-10 minutes or until tortillas are backed and turn golden.

Recipe notes:

1. You can add diced bell pepper (green, red, or both) in step 2.
2. You can adjust the spice levels by adding more curry powder or using chili powder instead of curry powder.

My Recipe Notes

Result: Loved it ♥   Okay ☑   Not for me ☒

Spice Level: Too Spicy 😖   Just Right 😊   Not Spicy Enough 😎

Date(s):

Comments:

SPICED CHICKEN TACOS

This recipe uses cooked or rotisserie chicken meat.

Ingredients

- 2 cups of rotisseries chicken meat – shredded or cut into pieces
- 1 tsp chili powder – divided
- ½ turmeric powder
- ½ tsp meat/garam masala (optional)
- ¼ cup red onions finely chopped
- ¼ cup cilantro chopped (optional)
- 1 cup Pico de Gallo or salsa
- 1 avocado, peeled, seeded and diced
- 1 tbsp olive oil
- 12 flour tortillas
- Salt to taste
- Lime wedges

Method

1. Sprinkle ½ tsp chili powder on the shredded chicken. Mix well and set aside.
2. Heat oil in a pan over medium heat, sauté onions, and spices.
3. Add chicken and mix well so the spices with hot oil sticks to chicken along with sautéed onions.
4. Warm tortillas, fill it with chicken from step 3, top with avocado, Pico de Gallo or salsa and cilantro and serve.

Recipe Notes:

1. If using fresh chicken, use 1 chicken breast diced into small pieces. Cook chicken in step 3 until golden brown and cooked through.
2. You could spice this up even further by adding jalapenos in step 2.
3. You can add garlic and ginger as well as turmeric powder in step 2.

My Recipe Notes

Result: Loved it ♥   Okay ☑   Not for me ☒

Spice Level: Too Spicy 😅   Just Right 🙂   Not Spicy Enough 😎

Date(s):

Comments:

_____

_____

_____

_____

_____

_____

_____

_____

_____

_____

_____

_____

_____

_____

_____

_____

CHAPTER 5. THAI INSPIRED SPICY CHICKEN RECIPES

Thai dishes can be really spicy and hot. Below are some Thai inspired dishes. You can experiment with these recipes by adjusting the amount of spices used.

THAI GREEN CURRY CHICKEN

Ingredients
- 1.5 lbs. boneless chicken breast or thighs cut into ½ inch pieces
- 1/2 cup Thai green curry paste
- 1 cup green beans (whole or cut into half)
- 1 cup broccoli
- 1 cup of coconut milk
- ½ inch ginger, sliced into long pieces
- ½ cup cilantro
- 2 tsp coconut (or vegetable) oil
- 1 sliced green chili
- Salt to taste
- 1 tsp lime juice

Method
1. Heat oil in a non-stick pan, add the green curry paste, green chilies, and ginger and fry it for 1-2 minutes stirring well.
2. Add chicken, beans, and broccoli. Mix well.
3. Add coconut milk; cover and cook for 15-20 minutes or the vegetables and chicken ate cooked. Add ½ -1 cup chicken broth if required.
4. Garnish with cilantro and serve with Jasmine rice.

Recipe Notes:

1. You can use the green curry paste made using the recipes given in my book "Beginner's Guide to Cooking with Spices" or buy off the shelf from Asian or online stores.

2. You can also add some lemongrass to enhance the flavor.

My Recipe Notes

Result: Loved it ♥   Okay ☑   Not for me ☒

Spice Level: Too Spicy 😆   Just Right 🙂   Not Spicy Enough 😎

Date(s):

Comments:

THAI MANGO CHICKEN CURRY

Mango is one of the most popular tropical fruits, especially in South Asian countries. Raw mango is used in many recipes, especially with fish. This recipe uses ripe mango and is almost like comfort food. This dish will tickle your taste buds with many flavors including sweetness, sour and spice.

Ingredients

- 2 lbs. chicken breast cut into small (1 inch) pieces
- 5 tbsp Thai red curry paste
- 1/2 tsp turmeric
- 2 medium onion chopped
- 2-3 tsp coconut oil
- ½ tsp pepper powder
- 1 tsp ginger paste or freshly grated ginger
- 3-4 garlic cloves minced
- 1 can coconut milk
- 1 fresh ripe mango peeled and cut (or 1 cup mango puree)
- 1 tsp fish sauce
- 1 tsp lime juice
- 2 kaffir lime leaves
- Salt to taste

Method

1. Sprinkle ½ tsp curry powder, turmeric, lime juice, and ¼ tsp salt on cut chicken. Mix well and keep it aside for 10 minutes.
2. In a separate pan, heat 2 tsp oil, add onions, garlic, and ginger. Sauté until onions become translucent.
3. Add Thai curry paste and sauté for another 1 minute.
4. Now transfer the sautéed onions and spices into a food processor or blender along with the mango chunks and blend until smooth
5. Heat 1 tsp oil to the same pan and add the marinated chicken and mix well for about 2 minutes so that any raw spices sticking to the chicken as marinade gets fried in oil and chicken is white outside.
6. Now add the spice and mango paste and coconut milk and mix well chicken pieces are well coated with mango and spice paste. Bring it to a boil. Now add kaffir lime leaves and fish sauce
7. Cover and cook for 12-15 minutes on low heat. Once the chicken is cooked, add salt to taste and mix. Switch off the heat and keep it covered for about 1-2 minutes before serving.

Garnish with coriander leaves and lime wedges. Serve with Jasmin rice or bread.

Recipe Notes:

1. Thai red curry paste is available in many of your local supermarket stores. You can also make your own Thai red curry paste at home. Please refer to my book "Introduction to Curry"
2. If fresh mango is not available, canned mango puree may be used.
3. If you are not a fan of mango, you could substitute mango with another cup of coconut milk.

My Recipe Notes

Result: Loved it ♥   Okay ☑   Not for me ☒

Spice Level: Too Spicy 😎   Just Right ☺   Not Spicy Enough 😎

Date(s):

Comments:

_____

_____

_____

_____

_____

_____

_____

_____

_____

_____

_____

_____

_____

_____

_____

THAI COCONUT CHICKEN CURRY NOODLE SOUP

Ingredients

- ½ lb. boneless chicken thighs or breast cut into small pieces
- 1 tbsp coconut oil
- 4 cloves of garlic chopped
- 1-inch ginger grated
- ¼ cup or 4 tbsp red curry paste
- 1 can (2 cups) of coconut milk
- 1-1/2 can (3 cups) of chicken broth
- ¼ cup Thai basil chopped
- 200 grams (7 oz) vermicelli rice noodles
- 2 tbsp fish sauce
- 1 medium tomato sliced
- ¼ cup cilantro
- 2 tsp lime juice (optional)
- Salt to taste
- Green onions chopped to garnish

Method

1. Heat oil in a large pan over medium heat, sauté ginger and garlic paste for about a minute. Add Thai red curry paste and fry for about 3-4 minutes.
2. Add chicken pieces and cook for another 5 minutes stirring well until chicken is coated with the curry paste and turns opaque.
3. Add chicken broth, coconut milk, fish sauce. Bring it to a boil. Taste and add salt if needed.
4. Add Thai basil. Mix. Now add the noodles. Bring it to a boil. Switch off and keep it covered for a couple of minutes. Add cilantro and optional lime juice and serve.

My Recipe Notes

Result: Loved it ♥   Okay ☑   Not for me ☒

Spice Level: Too Spicy 😊   Just Right ☺   Not Spicy Enough 😎

Date(s):

Comments:

EASY THAI RED CURRY CHICKEN

Ingredients
- 6-8 boneless chicken thighs cut into pieces
- 1 tbsp coconut oil
- 1 tbsp ginger-garlic paste
- ¼ cup or 4 tbsp red curry paste
- 2 cans of coconut milk
- ¼ cup Thai basil chopped
- ½ inch piece of ginger
- 2 Lime leaves

Method
1. Heat oil in a large pan over medium heat, sauté ginger-garlic paste for about a minute. Add Thai red curry paste and mix for another minute.
2. Add coconut milk and bring it a boil.
3. Add chicken and lime leaves. Bring to a boil and simmer covered for 10-15 minutes or until chicken is cooked.
4. Add Thai basil. Mix. Switch off the heat. Keep it covered for a couple of minutes before serving.

My Recipe Notes

Result: Loved it ♥   Okay ☑   Not for me ☒

Spice Level: Too Spicy 😆   Just Right 🙂   Not Spicy Enough 😎

Date(s):

Comments:

SPICY THAI BASIL CHICKEN

Ingredients
- 1 pound ground chicken
- 2 tbsp oil (coconut/vegetable/peanut)
- 1 tbsp crushed garlic
- 5-10 Thai chilies chopped up
- 1 can of coconut milk
- 1 cup Thai basil chopped
- ½ inch piece of ginger grated
- 1 teaspoon sriracha sauce
- 2 tsp soy sauce
- 2 tbsp fish sauce
- 2 Lime leaves

Method
1. Heat oil in a large pan over medium heat, sauté crushed garlic, ginger and chilies for about a minute. Add coconut milk and bring it a boil.
2. Add chicken and lime leaves. Bring to a boil and simmer covered for 10-15 minutes or until chicken is cooked.
3. Add Thai basil. Mix. Sprinkle sriracha sauce on top. Switch off the heat. Keep it covered for a couple of minutes before serving.

My Recipe Notes

Result: Loved it ♥ Okay ☑ Not for me ☒

Spice Level: Too Spicy 😵 Just Right 🙂 Not Spicy Enough 😎

Date(s):

Comments:

SPICY CHICKEN AND PINEAPPLE

Ingredients

- 1 pound boneless chicken breast cut into strips
- 2 tbsp oil (coconut/vegetable/peanut)
- 1 tbsp ginger-garlic paste
- ¼ cup Thai red curry paste
- 2 jalapenos slit (or Thai chili)
- 1 cans of coconut milk
- 1 cup sliced bamboo shoots
- ½ red bell pepper julienned
- ½ green bell pepper julienned
- 1 red onion chopped
- 1 cup Thai basil chopped
- 2 tbsp fish sauce
- 1 cup pineapple chunks

Method
1. Heat oil in a large pan over medium heat, sauté onions, garlic-ginger, and chilies for about 30 seconds. Add Thai curry paste, fish sauce, bamboo shoots, bell peppers and mix well.
2. Add coconut milk and bring it a boil.
3. Add chicken. Cook covered for 10-15 minutes or until chicken is cooked.
4. Add Thai basil and pineapple chunks. Mix. Switch off the heat. Keep it covered for a couple of minutes before serving.

My Recipe Notes

Result: Loved it ♥   Okay ☑   Not for me ☒

Spice Level: Too Spicy 😆   Just Right 🙂   Not Spicy Enough 😎

Date(s):

Comments:

THAI GINGER CHICKEN STIR-FRY

This is an easy recipe to make and the extra ginger is very good for your tummy as ginger is known for digestive health.

Basic Ingredients

- 1 lbs. boneless chicken breast or thighs cut into ½ inch pieces
- 3-4 tbsp fish sauce
- 1-2 tbsp oyster sauce
- 1-1/2 cup thinly sliced red bell pepper
- 1 cup green onions cut into 1-inch pieces
- ½ cup sliced onion
- 2 inches long ginger, cut into long matchstick shape
- 4-6 cloves of crushed garlic
- ½ cup cilantro
- 2 tsp coconut (or vegetable) oil
- Salt to taste
- 1 tbsp brown sugar

Method

1. Combine fish sauce, oyster sauce, and sugar in a bowl and set aside.
2. Heat oil in a large wok or skillet. Add oil. Now add chicken and let it sear for about 1 minute stirring so that both sides become lightly brown.
3. Add bell pepper, onions, ginger, garlic and the sauce combine and cook for 4-5 minutes or chicken is cooked through and bell pepper and onions are tender.
4. Garnish with cilantro and serve with Jasmine rice.

Recipe Notes:

1. You can add 1-2 chopped up jalapenos in step 3. This will increase the heat level a bit.

2. You can add 1 can coconut milk in step 3. In this case, you get Thai ginger chicken curry instead of stir-fry.

3. Add sliced up eggplant instead of bell pepper in step 3 as a variation to this recipe.

4. If you like to have it medium or Thai hot spice level, add 1-3 tsp Thai red chili paste in step 2.

5. If you like mushrooms, you may add chopped up mushrooms in addition to or instead of bell pepper in step 3.

My Recipe Notes

Result: Loved it ♥   Okay ☑   Not for me ☒

Spice Level: Too Spicy 😆   Just Right 🙂   Not Spicy Enough 😎

Date(s):

Comments:

CHAPTER 6. OTHER SPICY CHICKEN RECIPES

SPICY CHICKEN PIZZA

This is a recipe for making a spicy chicken pizza.

Ingredients

- 1 chicken breast cut into small slices
- 1 teaspoon ginger garlic paste
- 1 teaspoon of spice mix of your choice – garam masala or curry powder
- ½ - 1 teaspoon red chili powder
- Salt to taste
- ½ cup low-fat yogurt (optional)
- 10-12 pieces of pickled Jalapeno slices
- 1 cup of cheese blend (or ½ cup mozzarella, ½ cup cheddar)
- ¼ cup pizza sauce of your choice
- 1 large pizza base
- 2 tablespoons of olive oil
- ¼ cup chopped up bell pepper
- 1 spring onion chopped
- ¼ cup cilantro chopped (optional)

Method

1. Marinate chicken pieces in yogurt, salt, ginger-garlic paste and spices and set aside for 15 minutes (refrigerate for 2 hours or overnight if you have time)
2. Heat olive oil in a pan and cook the marinated chicken pieces mix well for even cooking on all sides.
3. If you are using a pre-made pizza base, spread the sauce of your choice, cheese blend and chicken from the pan evenly. Spread any spicy juices from cooking as well. Spread chopped up bell pepper and Jalapenos.
4. Bake at 400 degrees for 10 minutes. Garnish with chopped up spring onion and optional cilantro and enjoy.

Recipe notes:

1. Instead of yogurt to marinate, 1-2 tablespoon of lime juice may be used.
2. You may skip jalapenos depending on your spice tolerance level.
3. If you are using Pizza dough, you may need to roll it out and bake for 10 minutes prior to spreading the toppings to ensure the pizza base gets cooked well.
4. You can try with different pizza sauces both red and white sauces to vary the taste and experiment.
5. You can try different toppings in addition to spicy chicken to experiment:
   a. Green olives
   b. Spinach
   c. Bell peppers
   d. Onions
   e. Mushrooms
   f. Pineapple
   Each of these vegetables may be cooked along with chicken if you prefer in step 2 of the recipe above.

My Recipe Notes

Result: Loved it ♥   Okay ☑   Not for me ☒

Spice Level: Too Spicy 😵   Just Right 🙂   Not Spicy Enough 😎

Date(s):

Comments:

MORE EASY SPICY CHICKEN PIZZA RECIPE IDEAS

Below are a couple of more recipe ideas for spicy chicken pizza which are quick and easy.

1. Spicy Grilled Chicken Pita Pizza – Assemble a pizza using 1 pita bread, 1 tablespoon chili sauce, 2 tablespoon cheese and ¼ cup chopped up spicy grilled chicken.
2. Spicy Naan Pizza – Use an Indian Naan as the base and assemble using ingredients of your choice.
3. Try either pita bread pizza or naan pizza using salsa as the sauce – you can try mild, medium or hot salsa depending on your preference with spicy grilled/baked or curried chicken and cheese of your choice.

All these recipes are quick easy. Once assembled just bake for 5-10 minutes in an oven preheated to 400 degrees.

My Recipe Notes

Result: Loved it ♥   Okay ☑   Not for me ☒

Spice Level: Too Spicy 😆   Just Right 🙂   Not Spicy Enough 😎

Date(s):

Comments:

SPICY CHICKEN PASTA

This recipe is a fusion of Indian and Italian recipes.

Ingredients

- 1 chicken breast
- 1 lb. pasta penne
- ½ teaspoon ginger-garlic paste
- 1 teaspoon red chili powder
- ½ teaspoon turmeric powder
- ¼ cup nonfat yogurt
- Salt to taste
- 2 tablespoons of olive oil
- ¼ cup basil leaves
- ¼ cup green olives chopped
- ½ cup bell pepper chopped (any color)
- ¼ cup cherry tomatoes
- 1 onion sliced thinly
- 1 jalapeno cut into thin slices (optional)
- ¼ cup cilantro chopped (optional)

Method

1. Marinate chicken breast in yogurt, salt, ginger-garlic paste and half of the spices and set aside for 15 minutes (refrigerate for 2 hours or overnight if you have time)
2. Boil enough salted water in a pot and cook pasta for about 10 minutes. Drain and keep.
3. In parallel, bake or air fry or bake the marinated chicken at 400 degrees for 10 minutes. Once cooled down, cut the chicken into thin strips.
4. Heat oil in a large enough pan, sauté onions, add remaining spices, bell pepper, optional Jalapenos, olives, basil cherry tomatoes. Mix well and cook for about 4-5 minutes.
5. Add chicken and pasta. Mix well. Add optional Cilantro.

My Recipe Notes

Result: Loved it ♥   Okay ☑   Not for me ☒

Spice Level: Too Spicy 😅   Just Right 🙂   Not Spicy Enough 😎

Date(s):

Comments:

_____

_____

_____

_____

_____

_____

_____

_____

_____

_____

_____

_____

_____

_____

_____

_____

SPICY CHICKEN STEW

This recipe is one of the local dishes in the state of Kerala, India. This is a very creamy dish in coconut milk and goes with different kinds of Indian breads as well as other steamed rice/wheat dishes.

Ingredients

- 2 lbs. chicken thighs and legs bone-in
- 5-10 green chilies chopped
- ½ tsp cardamom
- 2-3 pieces of ½ inch cinnamon sticks
- 6-7 cloves
- 2 medium onion chopped
- 2-3 tsp coconut oil
- 2 tbsp ginger garlic paste (or 1 tbsp ginger paste and 1 tbsp garlic paste)
- 2 medium potatoes peeled and cut into cubes
- 1 cup green beans cut into 1-inch pieces
- 2 medium carrots cut into ½ inch pieces
- 2-3 medium tomatoes sliced
- Salt to taste
- 2 spring curry leaves
- 2 cans of coconut milk
- 3-4 tablespoon coconut oil or oil of your choice

Method

1. Heat oil in a large enough pan, fry the whole spices for about a minute and then add green chilies, onions, curry leaves, and ginger-garlic paste until onions become translucent.
2. Now add the chicken and vegetables and fry in the oil and spices for 2-3 minutes, stirring continuously.
3. Add coconut milk. Cover and cook until chicken and vegetables are cooked. Add salt to taste. Switch off the heat and keep it covered for about 1-2 minutes before serving.

Serve with naan or bread.

Recipe Notes:

1. You can make this dish an instant pot or pressure cooker. If using an instant pot, you can first use the sauté function and the cook in poultry setting or high pressure for about 10 minutes.
2. If you prefer, you can temper the stew using mustard seeds, whole red chilies, bay leaves, or curry leaves and additional whole spices. Tempering is an optional step and can be done for any of the curry recipes in this book.
3. You may have to dilute the coconut milk to cook if the store-bought cans of coconut milk is too thick. In this case dilute one can with same amount of water and use it for cooking. You may add the other thick coconut milk once the chicken is cooked.

My Recipe Notes

Result: Loved it ♥   Okay ☑ Not for me ☒

Spice Level: Too Spicy 😆 Just Right 🙂 Not Spicy Enough 😎

Date(s):

Comments:

Notes:

DISCLAIMER

This book details the author's personal experiences in using Indian spices, the information contained in the public domain as well as the author's opinion. The author is not licensed as a doctor, nutritionist, or chef. The author is providing this book and its contents on an "as is" basis and makes no representations or warranties of any kind with respect to this book or its contents. The author disclaims all such representations and warranties, including for example warranties of merchantability and educational or medical advice for a particular purpose. In addition, the author does not represent or warrant that the information accessible via this book is accurate, complete, or current. The statements made about products and services have not been evaluated by the US FDA or any equivalent organization in other countries.

The author will not be liable for damages arising out of or in connection with the use of this book or the information contained within. This is a comprehensive limitation of liability that applies to all damages of any kind, including (without limitation) compensatory; direct, indirect or consequential damages; loss of data, income or profit; loss of or damage to property and claims of third parties. It is understood that this book is not intended as a substitute for consultation with a licensed medical or a culinary professional. Before starting any lifestyle changes, it is recommended that you consult a licensed professional to ensure that you are doing what's best for your situation. The use of this book implies your acceptance of this disclaimer.

Thank You

If you enjoyed this book or found it useful, I would greatly appreciate if you could post a short review on Amazon. I read all the reviews and your feedback will help me to make this book even better.

Additional Notes & Observations on the Recipes

My favorite places to buy spices:

My favorite spice and why

Comments:

My Favorite Chicken Recipe

Write down or paste your favorite curry recipe below:

My Family Recipe

Source: Mom Dad Grandma Grandpa Other:

Write down or paste your family recipe below:

COOKING MEASUREMENTS AND CONVERSION CHARTS

Some of you may be using a different kitchen measurement system than described in the book. I believe most people can navigate these different systems. The following conversion tables included as a ready reference; in case you need it.

US Dry Volume Measurements	
Measurement	**Equivalent**
3 teaspoons	1 Tablespoon
¼ cup	4 Tablespoons
1/3 cup	5 1/3 Tablespoons
½ cup	8 Tablespoons
¾ cup	12 Tablespoons
1 cup	16 Tablespoons
1 Pound	16 ounces

US Liquid Volume Measurements and Conversion	
8 Fluid ounces	1 Cup
1 Pint	2 Cups (or 16 fluid ounces)
1 Quart	2 Pints (or 4 cups)
1 Gallon	4 Quarts (or 16 cups)

US to Metric Conversions	
1 teaspoon	5 ml
1 tablespoon	15 ml
1 fluid oz.	30 ml
1 cup	240 ml
2 cups (1 pint)	470 ml
4 cups (1 quart)	940 ml or approx. 1 litre
4 quarts (1 gal.)	3.8 liters or 16 cups
1 oz.	28 grams
1 pound (16 Oz.)	454 grams or approx. ½ kilo gram

Metric to US Conversions	
100 ml	3.4 fluid oz.
240 ml	1 cup

1 liter	34 fluid oz./ 4.2 cups/2.1 Pints/1.06 quarts/0.26 gallon
100 grams	3.5 ounces
500 grams	1.10 pounds
1 kilogram	2.205 pounds or 35 oz.

Oven Temperature Conversions	
Fahrenheit	**Celsius**
275° F	140° C
300° F	150° C
325° F	165° C
350° F	180° C
375° F	190° C
400° F	200° C
425° F	220° C
450° F	230° C
475° F	240° C

Printed in Great Britain
by Amazon